Crude Forecasts: Predictions, Pundits and Profits in the Commodity Casino

Peter Sainsbury

About the author

Peter Sainsbury is the author of *Commodities: 50 Things You Really Need To Know* and the founder of Materials Risk.

Acknowledgments

I would like to thank those industry experts who gave up their time and shared their insights - without which this book would be much the poorer. Thanks to Dr Angela Stokes (AcEDemy) for editing. Finally, I would like to thank my family, friends and colleagues for their time, ideas and patience.

"Forecasts are dangerous, particularly those about the future."

Sam Goldwyn

Contents

Preface 1

Chapter 1: The Future is Scary 7

Chapter 2: How Good are Commodity Forecasts? 15

Chapter 3: How to Forecast Commodity Prices 23

Chapter 4: The Economics of Commodities 41

Chapter 5: The Stories we Tell 57

Chapter 6: Pundits, Forecasters and Soothsayers 81

Chapter 7: The Illusion of Knowledge 93

Chapter 8: White Elephants 109

Chapter 9: Recommendations 133

Chapter 10: Conclusion 157

Preface

"Among all forms of mistake, prophesy is the most gratuitous."

George Eliot

A scandal that broke in the summer of 2008 was to have implications far from China's shores, arguably sparking a boom in the price of an essential commodity. A boom that eventually turned to bust.

Thousands of babies became sick with kidney stones after ingesting a chemical called melamine. Used to manufacture kitchen and bathroom counter-tops and dry-erase boards, melamine causes renal failure in humans. The chemical also happens to be rich in nitrogen, and so many Chinese farmers added it to the milk they collected to give the impression that it was rich in protein. Babies who were fed the tainted milk then suffered from protein deficiency; their mothers were unaware that the milk powder was not as described on the tin.

Chinese families, scared by the tainted product, looked for safe dairy options elsewhere. Countries as far away as the UK and Australia restricted the sale of infant formula. However, students, tourists, smuggling rings and canny entrepreneurs stocked up on the West's infant milk powder and then took it back to China or sold it through eBay-type websites in China.

For the farmers of New Zealand (the South Pacific nation is the world's biggest exporter of milk-based products), this was a big opportunity. It was a chance to capitalise on a short-term demand problem coming from its biggest consumer. But it was also the promise of never-ending demand for dairy products as Chinese consumers turned to more "Western" style diets.

Taking a product, assuming rising demand for it and multiplying that by 1.3 billion Chinese consumers can be a risky game. To meet China's insatiable demand for ice cream, infant formula and other dairy products, New Zealand's farmers ramped up production. They went on a buying spree, increasing their herds, purchasing land and converting sheep and beef farms to dairy. As of late 2013, many industry commentators were predicting dairy prices would continue to stay high, although perhaps a little weaker than the record prices.

Boom quickly turned to bust, however, when over the following 18 months dairy prices fell by almost 70%. China had purchased more milk than it needed, and when it found itself awash with milk the dairy exporters, such as those in New Zealand, bore the brunt of the pain, rather than China's domestic dairy industry. For many farming communities the situation became so desperate that some dairy farmers resorted to suicide, seeing no other way out from the collapse in milk prices, the impact on their incomes and the ability to support their families. The pain was felt right across an industry that stretches from the Pacific to Europe and North America and employs millions of workers.

The outlook for commodity prices is more than just of academic interest. This book is about predictions – why commodity markets are so difficult to forecast, the danger that forecasts may present and how we can all do better. It is about pundits – the bias present in forecasters and how to spot them. Finally, it is also about the pursuit of profit – by investors and all parts of the commodity supply chain.

Underpinning this book is fragility; of the food we eat, the materials we use for shelter and to sustain our standard of living and the energy we use to heat our homes. This book explains how you can make your life, your business and even the economy you work in less fragile. In the words of Nassim Nicolas Taleb, this book is about how to become more "anti-fragile".

The outlook for oil and other commodity markets are pored over for macroeconomic signals. Whether inflation will rear its head, whether a country's terms of trade might worsen and whether its energy companies, miners and farmers will see better returns in the months ahead. Prediction is indispensable to anyone involved in commodity markets. Every time you choose what car to buy, whether a farmer plants wheat or corn, whether a manufacturing company takes out a long-term energy contract or not, you are making a forecast about how the future will turn out.

This book has important lessons for how to view many other financial markets, how to interrogate their pundits and how to pick apart their predictions.

This book is for you, the investor.

As an investor, part of your portfolio is likely to include a significant share devoted to resource companies (miners, oil companies etc). So how can you make better decisions about where to devote your capital? This book will help you understand the challenges involved in forecasting commodity prices, providing you with a better list of questions to ask. It will help protect you from being sold a story which isn't backed up by reality.

To paraphrase a quote often attributed to Mark Twain, "A mine is a hole in the ground with a liar on top". This is too harsh a criticism of the sector, but it does illustrate my point that you, the investor, need to take companies to account for outlandish forecasts of future commodity prices.

This book is for you, the commodity producer.

As a current or prospective commodity producer, you want to attract investors to your business but it's important to spell out all of the risks involved. This book includes many recommendations for how you can do that. What questions should you be asking of the consultants that you've employed? How can you set the standard for the companies operating in the resource sector?

This book is for you, the consumer of commodities.

While your pension fund might have taken a hit, the average worker – you and me – now enjoy lower prices or at least ones that are not rising. However when the next boom in commodity prices comes (and it will – that is one forecast I can make), you, the consumer, will face rising costs and increasing fears over the supply of the materials that make your life and your business the way it is.

And this book is for government too.

Given the historical relationship between commodity prices and macroeconomic fluctuations, forward-looking policymakers and researchers have long been interested in predicting commodity price movements. Policymaking involves many considerations other than just price – security of supply, for example. Future taxpayers will not thank you if you've trapped them into paying high energy prices, way above the market rate, for long into the future. The incentives of government may be different, but that doesn't mean you shouldn't ask the difficult questions regarding the future risks to commodity prices.

I also hope that this book will be a spur to change.

Trust in "experts" of all sorts has been eroded in recent years, and before trust can be restored we sometimes need to look to ourselves to make marginal or more fundamental improvements. Despite being studied by some of the highest-paid analysts on Earth, commodity markets confound with maddening regularity.

It is amusing to poke fun at the experts when their forecasts fail. It's easy for a book about forecasts to say look at so and so's forecast and, here, look how wrong it is. And there will be some of that in this book. However, lets be careful with our schadenfreude. To say our forecasts are better than the experts' is to damn ourselves with some faint praise. However, we can all do better, improving our own forecasts while also holding the pundits to account.

Forecasters are often likened to a car, being driven by a local with knowledge of an isolated winding road smothered in fog. The driver is being followed by others at a safe distance; the lead driver signalling to those behind where the twists and turns in the road are so that followers don't crash into a tree or fall over a cliff.

I think this is an interesting if flawed analogy. How do you know the driver in front knows what he is doing? Will you, like sheep, just follow him over the same said cliff? The analogy also implies that commodity forecasters have some kind of omnipotent power to see ahead and prevent one or another market from teetering too far away from its fundamentals. Commodity markets and the track record of forecasters suggest that this is not the case. As with following a car in the fog, don't just follow commodity forecasts blindly. The experience of the farmers in New Zealand shows that the outlook for commodity prices is more than just an academic interest – it has real consequences.

This book will help you understand the challenges and biases facing the commodity forecaster and, therefore, it will help you ask better questions to bring them to account.

Above all, I hope this book will help you make better decisions. Better decisions on what investments to make. Better decisions on what crop to farm. Better decisions on how to get the best deal for your business.

Chapter 1: The Future is Scary

"An uncertain future leaves us stranded in an unhappy present with nothing to do but wait."

Daniel Gilbert

The year was 2011. For the second time in less than four years the price of wheat, corn and other agricultural commodities had risen sharply. Agricultural prices had rocketed to the highest level in real terms for almost three decades.

The rising cost of food had played a role in provoking uprisings against several authoritarian regimes, while adding millions to the number who go to bed hungry each night. Companies sounded the alarm and the world's largest economies put "food security" at the top of their to-do list.

A confluence of factors led to the spike in food prices, such as drought in Russia and Argentina, floods in Canada and Pakistan and high oil prices. A weak US dollar and an increased consumption of grains and other agricultural commodities from China, India and other emerging economies also spurred demand. But what made the crisis worse was panic.

A study by the Food and Agricultural Organization (FAO) of the United Nations (UN) found that over thirty nations – including Russia, Ukraine and Argentina – introduced bans on the export of agricultural products. The aim of these measures was to insulate their citizens from the sharp increase in prices and to make sure there was enough food to go round. This was entirely rational from the perspective of governments worried about the reaction of their citizens to higher food prices. However, these export bans, coupled with panic buying by importers spooked into restocking their grain reserves, helped fuel the spike in prices.[1]

Few things matter to basic human existence more than the yields of staple crops such as wheat and corn. Until very recent history, the struggle to provide enough food to eat was the focus of much of human activity. Starvation was an ever-present threat because even the best years rarely yielded much of a surplus to carry over as an insurance against leaner times. In the worst years, only the rich and powerful could be sure of a full stomach.

Fear of food scarcity is a recurring theme throughout history, with doomsayer's always willing to predict catastrophe. In the late 1800s, Thomas Robert Malthus thought that famine, disease and war were necessary to bring the number of people back in line with the capacity to feed them. As recently as the 1970's, Paul Ehrlich and many other commentators believed that overpopulation would cause disaster, that billions would die, that developed countries would disintegrate and that India was beyond saving, etc.

Fast forward to the present day and while concerns over shortages of many commodities – from corn to cobalt and from lead to lithium – continue to be a feature of modern life in the early twenty-first century, oil is the current primary driver of our fears for the future. Volatility in the price of the world's most essential commodity is perilous. It causes tax revenues for countries that heavily rely on the export of crude oil to swell and shrink unpredictably, and it spreads uncertainty to every sector of the global economy that relies on affordable transportation. Uncertainty over the price of crude oil and its availability pervades our entire economic system.

Humans don't like uncertainty, especially when it comes to the most basic requirements to sustain us. And so, since Man's first existence, we have tried to see patterns in the sun, wind, rain and stars. We have created rules of thumb for what tomorrow's weather will bring, and whether God or other omnipotent powers above would unleash a storm or an earthquake. All of which we hope will tell us what tomorrow will bring, whether we will have enough food to last us the winter.

As with commodity markets as it is in all areas of life, we just can't live without some kind of prediction. All decisions reflect some view of the future, even if it's a sense that things will be much like they are now – that too is a forecast.

In the face of such uncertainty we have often turned to others who we believe have the knowledge, expertise and skills to look to the future and warn us whats on the horizon. These soothsayers continue to be in demand today.

So who uses commodity predictions and what are their incentives? Typically commodity predictions are used by four distinct groups; governments and central banks; producers of raw materials (eg, an oil exploration company); manufacturers and investors.

Governments and central banks

In a June 2008 speech, titled "Outstanding Issues in the Analysis of Inflation", US Federal Reserve Chairman Ben Bernanke singled out the role of commodity prices among the main drivers of price dynamics. In turn, he underscored the importance for economic policy of both accurate forecasting of commodity price changes and understanding the factors that drive those changes.[2]

Indeed, uncertainty over the future price of oil is thought to be one of the main causes of uncertainty in inflation projections – complicating decisions over future monetary and fiscal policy. Work by the European Central Bank found that a 20% change in the oil price can affect inflation by approximately 0.4-0.8 percentage points (depending on the initial level of the oil price).[3]

Why is this important for policymakers? Well, when a central bank sets the level of interest rates, they know it may take 18-24 months before the impact is seen in the economy. If, based in part on their expectations for future oil prices they think inflation will rise over the next year then they may decide to increase interest rates to stop inflation from filtering through the economy. If they are wrong and inflation doesn't rise as much as feared, then they will have unduly stymied economic growth.

Producers of raw materials

The outlook for commodity prices are also important for companies that supply commodities. Forecasts of the trajectory of prices over the next few months and years will drive decisions affecting billions of dollars of investment in commodity production. One of the first things an intelligent asset allocator must do is make expected return forecasts for the commodity producing assets that they own. However, volatile commodity prices make it difficult for long-term investors to assess both a company's current value and its future value.

This is a particular risk when you consider junior mining and energy exploration projects. These projects can be perilous, often taking place in inhospitable and unstable parts of the world. An optimistic (frequently sky high) price trajectory is generally used to justify the risk that investors are taking. This may leverage billions of dollars worth of capital, but at high risk. Even if the mine operators are successful in bringing a product to market, investors may still be disappointed with the future payoff.

While the outlook for commodity prices influences how billions of dollars are invested in grand projects, it also affects how individual farmers spend their much more meagre but no less important amounts of money, capital and hard work. Therefore, the outlook for agricultural commodity prices is extremely important for farmers. If the farmer is wrong, then he may have toiled away at the land or nurtured his livestock for many years only to find a glut when it's ready for market. He may then have to resort to storage or, worse, the produce being wasted.

Take the example of a sugar cane farmer. He will do what everyone else does. First, he will take the current price as a reference and then try to work out what factors could move the price up or down over the coming months and years to the point at which he expects to harvest. Second, the farmer might talk to neighbouring farms – how much are they growing this season and what, therefore, is the risk of oversupply? All in all, he gathers as much evidence as he can, including taking the views of commodity forecasters, to help him decide how much to plant.

That is only one part of the equation, however. The farmer will also have to take a view on what the future cost of fertiliser and harvesting will be. Will oil prices rise? If it does then it will also increase the price of fertiliser and the cost of running harvesting machines.

Manufacturers

Processors and manufacturers also need to take a view on the price of their main raw material. Commodities are generally not produced for their own sake, but for the products that can be manufactured from them. Take the example of sugar again. Both sugar cane and sugar beet need processing in a factory before the sugar can be consumed. By agreeing to buy sugar cane or beet from a farmer, the factory owner is hoping to sell the sugar it refines from it at a profit. The owner needs to form an opinion as to how much they should sell forward and how much they should leave until the sugar is produced.

Not all manufacturers have the same incentive to understand the factors affecting their raw materials. For some firms, materials may only be a small percentage of their overall costs or they may be reliant on several raw materials, reducing the time they can allocate to analysing each commodity market. Meanwhile, they may be one of many end customers for a particular commodity producer, reducing the impact they may have in negotiating terms.

The typical end consumer, you and I, at least subconsciously rely on forecasts in forming expectations over whether fuel prices will be cheap or expensive. For instance, this may affect your decision when you come to buy a new car. Do you buy a small fuel-efficient car or a gas-guzzler?

Investors

The outlook for commodity prices is important to investors in commodities and the companies exposed to them, but it also affects all investors no matter what asset they invest in. To understand why remember that no economic variable is more important to investors than inflation. The outlook for inflation affects the performance of equity markets, government bonds, currencies and many other financial assets. Conventional wisdom is that inflation is directly related to how much money the central bank prints. American economist Milton Friedman said: "Inflation is always and everywhere a monetary phenomenon."

Yet a better guide to inflation (at least when looking out over the period of a year) has been the price of commodities. Swings in oil markets and the market expectations of long-term inflation have moved in lockstep. Arend Kapteyn, Chief Economist of the investment bank UBS, calculates that 84% of the variation in US inflation since 2002 is explained by shifts in oil and food prices.[4]

Commodity forecasts are often used to decide on what positions to take in commodity futures and what investments to make in commodity producers' equities. Often prices may jump after a bullish forecast is published, because traders bid up prices in the expectation that other traders and investors will do likewise. However, that poses risks to the investor. He or she will not know if the person or institution providing the forecast has any "skin-in-the-game" and, even if they do, if it may change in the days, weeks and months ahead. There is no guarantee that the forecaster will tell you that their view of the market has changed.

The information vacuum present in commodity markets creates a strong incentive to seek those who we perceive as having access to superior data and insight. What do we do when the future is so uncertain and so much rides on it? We look to the experts. Dan Gardner, in his book "Future Babble: Why Expert Predictions

Fail – And Why We Believe Them Anyway", highlights how turning to someone who will provide you with a forecast is half the battle: "Expert predictions do away with complexity, incomprehension, and uncertainty. In their place was the gentle buzz of knowing. All one needed to do was to pick an expert and listen." The simple act of having something to hang on to provides the basis for action.[5]

For the farmer, this means that he can feel that he is making a rational decision on what crop to plant next season. For the investor, it may be another part of the narrative he can use to inform or justify his retirement investment decisions. For others, such as the managers of our biggest companies, the forecasts may help to justify billions of dollars of investment.

Gardner goes onto say that rejecting the pseudo certainty of experts' predictions is a scary prospect for most people: "And if you do that – and you can't accept superstition, religion, or conspiracy theories – what are you left with? Nothing. And that's frightening."

But would you trust an expert without a track record? Would you trust a doctor without any certificates to diagnose your ailments, a dentist who had no track record of pulling teeth, or even a financial advisor who could not demonstrate that he had the best interests of his clients at heart? I wouldn't! So how can you trust financial market pundits as if they are some kind of oracle without first analysing their track record? The next chapter provides the first step in restoring that trust.

Chapter 2: How Good are Commodity Forecasts?

"Economists don't forecast because they know, they forecast because they're asked."

J. K. Galbraith, economist

Let's get straight to the meat of the issue. If the predictions of future commodity prices were accurate, then there wouldn't be a case for writing this book. So before we go any further, it's worth asking how good are they?

The *Wall Street Journal* (WSJ) polls institutions every month on a range of economic variables including inflation, unemployment and West Texas Intermediate (WTI) crude oil prices. Each month, the survey asks for predictions for the forthcoming June and December. For the sake of consistency, I have reviewed the accuracy of forecasts made both six and 12 months prior to June and December each year. I reviewed surveys from mid-2007 to the end of 2016 and so this covered booms and busts, financial crises and quantitative easing, the Arab Spring and the shale revolution.[6]

By means of a disclaimer, this is not an exhaustive study. By definition, it only covered a ten year period, and there is no guarantee that forecasters that were correct during this boom and bust period will be any more or less successful in future periods. It also says nothing about how well those same institutions did trying to predict other commodity prices including metal and agricultural prices. Finally, it only covers those forecasters that the WSJ surveyed – there may have been others who were more or less accurate in their predictions.

Using this data (available to view at materials-risk.com/crudeforecasts), I tried to answer the following three questions: were the forecasts correct?; were the predictions valuable?, and, third, was there a forecaster that you could have followed that would have led to a better overall result than taking the consensus? Let's discuss each of these points in more detail.

First, were the forecasts right? The answer was clearly no. The average consensus forecast (ie, the average of the commodity price predictions) for WTI crude oil was off by 27% when forecasting six months out. Oil price forecasts looking twelve months out were only slightly worse, off by an average of 30%. Another way of looking at it is that only in three of the nineteen periods reviewed was the consensus six month forecast within 5% of the actual result.[7]

As noted earlier, producers, manufacturers, investors and traders are making billions of worth of investment based on the outlook for commodity prices. If these forecasts are awry on as short term a time period as twelve months then how can they have confidence making decisions over much longer time periods?

Second, did any of the forecasts spot the major changes in the direction of the oil price over the past decade? In June 2008, WTI crude was trading at approximately $135 per barrel. The consensus prediction for December 2008 was just under $112 per barrel and $101 per barrel twelve months ahead. The reality was somewhat different. The financial crisis hit and with it the oil price was hit too. WTI crude prices fell to $41 per barrel in late December 2008, only rebounding to $70 per barrel in mid-2009. Almost all forecasters polled in mid-2008 saw prices falling over the next twelve months, but no one saw the scale of the collapse. The closest six month forecast, although over 50% higher than the outcome, came from Parsec Financial Management!

It was a similar story in trying to call the rebound in prices. Remember that oil and other commodities rebounded in 2009 as quantitative easing helped support prices. Back in December 2008, however, the consensus prediction for June 2009 was for prices to stay low, only nudging up from the current levels of the time. This time the consensus was over 30% too low. Only three forecasts called the market within 5%: Societe Generale, Barclays and the Economic and Revenue Forecast Council.

Over the next few years, oil prices traded in a gradually narrowing range between $70 and $110 per barrel. Sure enough, the consensus and individual forecasts, increasingly anchored against recent prices, turned out to be broadly correct - well at least within a range of 5-15%. Like many forecasters, these economists were driving with their eyes fixed on the rear view mirror, enabling them to tell us where things were but not where they were going. This bears out the old adage that "it's difficult to make accurate predictions, especially with regard to the future." The corollary is also true: predicting the past is a snap.

If we fast forward to June 2014, oil prices were trading at approximately $105 per barrel, having peaked at just over $112 per barrel ten months earlier. The consensus forecast was for oil prices to fall from those levels to below $99 per barrel in December 2014. In reality, the consensus proved too optimistic by 85%. All of the forecasters were over 65% too optimistic, apart from one - Parsec Financial Management had predicted oil prices to be in the late $60s per barrel range in December 2014, only 24% too high.

Does that mean that Parsec Financial Management have superior insight? Well, not quite. A look back through earlier forecasts reveals that they were consistently bearish all the way back to early 2010, calling for oil prices to stay around $50-70 per barrel, even though oil prices kept on rising. This is what's known as the "stopped watch" method of prediction. If you keep on saying something extreme will happen and it eventually does then you are feted as a guru when, in reality, you were lucky (eventually) with the timing.

Predictions are most useful when they anticipate change. If you predict that something will stay the same and it doesn't change, that prediction is unlikely to earn you much money or wow clients with your predictive abilities. However, predicting change can be very profitable for investors, while timing hedging strategies can be a welcome boost to both producers and manufacturers.

Third, was there a forecaster that you could have followed that would have led to a better overall result than taking the consensus? Of those 26 institutions that contributed prices for at least 14 of the 19 forecast periods *and* during the key turning points in the market identified above, three forecasters achieved a better than average result than the consensus when looking over a period of six months. These were: JP Morgan (26% forecast error, 4 correct calls); Comerica Bank (25%, 2) and The Conference Board (25%, 3). The most accurate institution achieved a two-percentage point improvement on the consensus, but still had an average six-month forecasting error of well over 20%. The research sample also includes Goldman Sachs, often famed for its supposed commodity prediction ability. How did they do? They were an average of 36% off with one correct call.

"The lucky idiot"

Nevertheless, the ability to predict, over very short periods says little about the quality of a forecast. As with investment success in the stock market, or anywhere else, it's very difficult to measure success in retrospect or a priori. If someone you follow correctly predicts the price of oil, it looks good on paper, but what you can't gleam from the magic number is what the risk was that it didn't happen. To what extent was the forecaster a "lucky idiot", as the investor Nassim Nicholas Taleb would call them?

That a forecast for future oil prices turns out right doesn't mean it was bound to happen. Howard Marks, manager of Oaktree Capital, uses the example of the weatherman to explain:[8]

> He says there's a 70 percent chance of rain tomorrow. It rains; was he right or wrong? Or it doesn't rain; was he right or wrong? It's impossible to assess the accuracy of probability estimates other than 0 and 100 except over a very large number of trials.

But the climate and the weather are never the same on any one day. A meteorologist can look back at similar patterns and infer what is likely to happen tomorrow. Commodity forecasters can do a similar exercise too, but it will never be the same. The world is always changing.

Risk exists only in the future, and it's impossible to know for sure what it holds. No ambiguity is evident when we view the past. Only the things that happened, happened. That definiteness, however, doesn't mean the process that creates outcomes is clear-cut and dependable. Many things could have happened, and the fact that only one happened devalues the variability that existed.

Remember, predictions are made with foresight, but tested with hindsight. It is easy to look back at a sequence of events that led to a forecast turning out correct and to lead the pundit, and anyone who had seen that forecast, to say: "I knew it would, it was obvious it would turn out that way." The hindsight bias, as it's known, prevents the forecaster and the consumer of that forecaster from reviewing whether it was correct because the pundit judged the risks correctly, or whether the pundit was just a "lucky idiot".

The pundit (or lucky idiot) might be infamous for making one big call. But is that enough? Given enough events, even a monkey can make the right prediction eventually. Does that mean that the monkey is endowed with magical powers of insight about the future? Sadly no. For purely statistical reasons, outstanding performances tend to be followed by something less impressive. This is because most performances involve some randomness. On any given day, the worst observed outcomes will be incompetents having an unlucky day, and the best observed outcomes will be stars having a lucky day. Observe the same group on another day and, because luck rarely lasts, the former outliers will not be quite as bad, or as good, as they first seemed.

Regression to the mean, as it's known, probably explains why many winners subsequently disappoint. And the disappointment will be spectacular if some people are taking bigger risks than others. The most impressive performance may combine skill with luck. In a financial market — or a casino — the easiest way to become an outlier is to make a big bet.

While randomness can explain much, hubris may also play a role. The economists Ulrike Malmendier of University of California, Berkeley and Geoffrey Tate of University of California, Los Angeles examined what happened to companies whose chief executives won accolades such as *Forbes*'s "Best Performing CEO" or *BusinessWeek*'s "Best Manager". They picked a statistical control group of near-winners who might have been expected to win an award, but did not.⁹

Like the near-winners, the winners ran large and profitable companies. However, those companies run by the winners did far worse in the three years following the award, lagging behind the near-winners by approximately 20%. The prizewinning CEOs, nevertheless, enjoyed millions of dollars more in pay. They were also more likely to write books, accept seats on other corporate boards and improve their golf handicap.

Chapter 3: How to Forecast Commodity Prices

"The world is too complex for that. We can analyze trends, we can give some probabilities — we can't really predict the future."

Seth J. Masters, chief investment officer of Bernstein Private Wealth Management

In order to understand the risks inherent in different forecasts it is important to delve under the hood. In this chapter I look at the different methods by which forecasters hope to predict commodity prices. The main methods used to help forecast prices include futures prices, fundamentals, the cost of production, the exchange rates of commodity-exporting countries, technical analysis, hotellings rule and finally todays price. This list is not exhaustive and by their nature are often used in combination with other methods and used in different ways over short and long-term forecasting periods.

Futures prices as a predictor

Futures prices are often used in the macroeconomic models built by central banks and other official agencies, and it is tempting to view them as a commodity price forecast. To recap, futures markets provide a means for trading the price of a commodity for delivery at some point in the future. The shape of this series of prices is known as the futures curve. The notion that the futures price is the best forecast of the spot price comes from a belief in the so-called "Efficient Market Hypothesis". In an efficient market, new information is instantly reflected in commodity prices.

The two terms "futures" and "forecast" both

sound like they should represent the same thing. They are anything but. A cursory review of the futures curve's behaviour in recent years shows that it has been a very poor predictor of realised spot commodity prices. The futures curve shows the price at which it is possible to buy or sell contracts for a date in the future at a price agreed on today. It is not a forecast of future spot prices.[10]

A futures curve is described as being "in contango" when it is upward sloping and so prices in six months' time are higher than the spot price. This is also known as a normal curve or a normal market. Traders will pay a premium to avoid the costs associated with transporting, storing and insuring a commodity (known as the cost to carry); so, the furthest-out contracts are typically higher in price. In contrast, when the shape of the futures price curve is downward sloping, then the market is said to be in backwardation. This is also called an inverted curve or an inverted market.

Forecasters may view a rising futures curve (a market in contango) as a sign that the market expects higher prices, and vice versa for a downward sloping futures curve. This is based on the perception that futures prices should incorporate all the available information to market participants, and that they also act as signals of what the "market" expects to happen.

There are several factors that affect the futures curve, not just market expectations of where the price of a commodity will be. First, the physical characteristic of the commodity – whether it is easy to store and whether there are ample inventories, etc. Second, longer dated contracts are illiquid, raising doubts of whether they are an effective aggregator of information. Third, the futures curve fails to account for inflation. The fourth and final factor is that futures prices will always be discounted to the market's expected future spot price in order to give investors a "risk premium" to take on risk from producer hedgers (known as the "normal backwardation" theory). This means that even if the spot price is estimated correctly, the traded futures price will tend to understate the market's current real price expectations.

Remember that commodity markets are characterised by frequent ruptures in the dominant price trend and that futures prices are of no use at all in forecasting these breaks in the trend. In addition, although some of the major commodities have well developed and liquid futures markets, this is not the case for all commodities. Nevertheless, forecasts by government institutions are likely to continue to use the futures curve. Why? It is because it is a simple and transparent market-based measure and so it is preferable to the more opaque model-based forecasts.

Menzie Chinn and Olivier Coibion, writing in the *Journal of Futures Markets*, looked at the overall efficiency and predictive ability of commodity futures markets. Using data from 1990, the researchers found that overall, energy and agricultural futures prices have much better predictive capability than precious and base metals. Within the energy sector, the report found that crude futures markets do not predict subsequent price changes as well as other energy futures markets, such as natural gas and gasoline. There is a similar situation in agricultural markets, with corn and soybean futures markets found to have a much better predictive power than wheat.[11]

As a whole, however, the overall predictive ability of commodity futures curves has declined since the mid-2000s. Chinn and Coibion believe this may have something to do with the increased financialisation of commodity markets, which has increased the degree of co-movement in futures prices.

Fundamentals as a predictor

Constructing a supply and demand balance of current fundamentals and then adjusting them up or down over the outlook period is one way that institutions attempt to quantitatively predict whether a commodity market will be in deficit or surplus in the future. In this simple approach, forecasters might look in isolation at a number of economic variables to gauge what impact they have had on demand and supply in the past, and then adjust accordingly based on the forecaster's expectations for the future. This can be a risky approach. Since commodity markets are characterised by price inelastic demand and supply, even small revisions in the expected path of future supply and demand can have large and volatile effects on prices.

Alternatively, forecasters typically rely on more complex data-based models to forecast commodity demand and supply. Models analyse the relationship between thousands of economic variables, from industrial production, business and consumer confidence data, retail sales volumes, money aggregates, and interest rates, data on inventories and production of industrial metals and energy commodities.

In a paper published in 1995, Greg Mankiw of Harvard University argued that the data-based approach faces insurmountable statistical problems – too many things happen at once to isolate cause and effect. For example, trade liberalisation might boost demand growth; governments might encourage trade liberalisation when economic growth is strong; or both liberalisation and growth might follow from some third unknown factor. There are also too many potential influences to know whether a strong relationship between variables is real or would disappear if they factored in some other relevant titbit of information.[12]

In addition, the risk with models like these is that they are too deterministic in nature. As I outline in Chapter 5 markets are much more complex than this, exhibiting positive and negative feedback loops. Models just focused on supply and demand, without accounting for how markets react to price signals may give an unrealistic picture of future market imbalances. Furthermore, supply and demand projections imply that each is known with equal precision, whereas in reality each will have been estimated with varying degrees of risk and uncertainty.

According to researchers at the Federal Reserve Bank of New York, forecasting models based on large panels of global economic variables can help, but their predictive properties are by no means overwhelming.[13]

The timeline of the forecast matters. When used to forecast one month and one quarter ahead, economic models provide significantly better predictions than a basic autoregressive or random walk benchmarks (ie, assuming that recent past prices are a good guide for future prices).[14]

However, when the forecasting horizon is six months or longer, the forecast performance of economic models does no better than these crude methods. When the researchers added commodity futures prices into their models, there was little evidence of any improvement over the original economic model.

The cost of production as a predictor

Over the long term, the cost of production is thought by many to represent the best gauge for future commodity prices. Jim O'Neil, previously of Goldman Sachs, advocated this approach:[15]

> In my ongoing quest to become better at forecasting, I began, a few years ago, to pay attention to the five-year forward oil price as it compares to the Brent crude oil spot price, the price of a barrel of oil today. I suspect that the five-year forward price is much less influenced by speculation in the oil market than the spot price, and more representative of true commercial needs. So when the five-year price starts moving in a different direction than the spot price, I take notice.

In the short term, the cyclical part of oil prices is determined by fluctuations in short-term fundamentals, as captured by inventory levels. As demand adjusts over short time horizons, demand is the most important driver of the cyclical part of price and it dominates the market on a 1-2 year horizon.

Given the capital and time intensive nature of commodity production investments, supply is typically slower to adjust than demand. Structural supply side factors typically drive the market on a 2-10 year horizon. These are determined by the long-term supply curve or the cost of bringing the last needed unit of the commodity to the market – referred to as the marginal cost of production. Throughout the 1980s and 1990s, long-dated crude futures prices rarely moved, reflecting the stable cost of bringing new supply into the market. Things changed from about 2004 as Chinese demand, in particular, made itself felt.

Several factors influence the cost of producing a commodity, including: geology, other commodity prices, geopolitics, resource nationalism and not to mention the main development costs. Since these factors are also in a constant state of flux, the marginal cost of production is too – it is a moving target.

Remember though that prices can, and frequently do fall below both average and marginal cost levels for considerable periods of time. Even if a particular mine is operating at a loss, there is a good chance it will continue to operate. This is because it costs a significant amount of money to close and eventually re-open a mine – so producers will tend to keep operating it for much longer than they would ideally want to. Once the initial investment has been made the incentive remains to continue producing as long as the price remains above the project's operating cost. This will usually be much lower than the breakeven rate or marginal cost of production.

As with the discussion on the problem with futures curves, this approach falls down with the same problems (ie, it tells you very little about the risk of large changes in price trends). Again, it should be used with caution, as a guide alongside other information.

The exchange rates of commodity-exporting countries as a predictor

Some market observers believe that the exchange rate fluctuations of commodity-exporting economies – such as Australia, Chile or South Africa – are privileged predictors of future global commodity prices. Primary commodity products represent significant components of output in the above-mentioned countries, affecting a large fraction of their export earnings. Changes in the global commodity price of copper and iron ore represent significant external shocks for Chile and Australia, respectively. Therefore, their exchange rates should, in theory, move today in anticipation of the future terms of trade adjustment.

Why the exchange rate of a commodity producer should be a better predictor of the future direction of the price than the underlying commodity is open to question, however. Just as the share price of a mining company that extracts copper is not just affected by the price of copper (think of the quality of the management, cash flow and costs, etc), then the factors affecting a country that exports a lot of copper (Chile, for example) is also affected by lots of different factors (such as whether the country has sound fiscal and monetary policy and whether its government is stable).

As commodity prices may experience periods where the price sways from the underlying fundamentals, that is also true of share prices and currencies that are exposed to commodities too. Note, also, that the commodity composition of many of these commodity producers is changing. Australia, for example, has been heavily dependent on the export of iron ore, but is now building up its exports of Liquid Natural Gas (LNG). As exports of LNG rise to rival or even overtake exports of iron ore, how then are the market expectations of the future price of the two commodities disentangled by solely looking at the exchange rate?[16]

According to the NBER there is limited evidence that commodity currencies are useful predictors of commodity prices. Commodity currencies typically do relatively well as a predictor over a very short-term horizon (say one quarter ahead), although not as well as economic models.[17]

Technical analysis as a predictor

Many commodity futures speculators and forecasters base their analysis of the likely future path of commodity prices on technical analysis, ignoring underlying fundamentals. Physical buyers and sellers of commodities are increasingly using technical analysis to help guide their decisions. Technical analysis involves looking at the past performance of commodity prices to predict or at the least point to the potential risk of future price movements. Technical analysis contradicts the Efficient Market Hypothesis, because it means that future movements in commodity prices can be 'predicted', to some degree at least based on historical price movements.

Why do traders and market analysts still use technical analysis if economic theory, at least, suggests that it shouldn't work? Some argue that there are too many unknowns to predict future physical supply and demand for a particular commodity. And they argue that, even if they could, the correlation between price and the physical fundamentals is too loose to be of any use.

The power of belief goes some way in explaining why technical analysis appears to work at least part of the time. Jonathan Kingsman, in his book "The Sugar Casino", argues that although individual human beings are irrational and emotional, group behaviour becomes repeatable and predictable. Humans use their experiences of past events to show them how to react to current ones. With enough technical traders with sufficient collective experience of the market, you might get repeatable price patterns. With enough repeatable price patterns, you might be able to forecast the future price of a commodity just by looking at the pattern.[18]

One argument against using technical analysis rests on what the method is based on – the price. It's hard to put a price on an asset that doesn't produce income. It's hard to say what the right price is for a commodity like oil and, thus, when the price is too high or too low. Was it too high at $100-plus? Was it an unsustainable blip? History says "no": it was that price for 43 consecutive months leading to August 2014. And if it wasn't too high then, is it too low today? The answer is that you can't say. Ditto for whether the response of the price of oil to the changes in fundamentals has been appropriate, excessive or insufficient. And if you can't be confident about what the right price is now, then you can't be definite about whether the price was correct six months ago, a year ago or ten years ago.

Researchers at the Copenhagen Business School sought to work out whether technical analysis has any long lasting predictive power. They looked at three methods used in technical analysis: moving averages, rate of change and the relative strength index (RSI). First, technical analysts might take the near term futures price rising above the 200 day moving average as a sign that prices will continue to increase. Second, the rate of change in the price of a commodity from one period to the next might indicate whether that trend will continue or not. An acceleration points towards a trend continuing and, in contrast, a deceleration is thought to show that a trend is coming to an end. Third, and finally, RSI shows whether a market is overbought or oversold, possibly showing that the trend will reverse.[19]

The Copenhagen researchers applied these three methods to the price series for four metals (aluminium, copper, zinc and tin) over the twenty years to 2013. The paper finds that technical analysis, at least using the methods described, has no consistent predictive power. A technical analyst would argue that they don't use one method of technical analysis, that the methods used in this analysis are far from sophisticated and that it's all about spotting the right opportunity rather than being in the market all the time. Nevertheless, the research argues that relying on rudimentary forms of technical analysis alone is not enough to forecast commodity prices consistently.

Hotelling's rule as a predictor

Hotelling's rule states that the most profitable extraction path for a non-renewable resource is one along which the price of the commodity, determined by the marginal net revenue from its sale, increases at the rate of interest. To use oil as an example, if a producer believed that prices would not keep up with higher interest rates, they would be better off selling as much as possible for cash and purchasing bonds. Conversely, if they expected that crude prices would increase faster than the prevailing interest rate, they would be better off keeping the oil in the ground and waiting for a higher price. Hotelling's rule suggests that over the long term, at least, output will rise at a rate that means the oil price will only increase at the rate of interest.

Analysis by the Bank of England examined the relative performance of Hotelling's rule in forecasting the price of oil. They compared it with the futures price, a consensus forecast (based on the average prediction from a number of financial institutions) and a random walk (taking the current spot price as the predictor). Looking at how well these different methods did at forecasting oil prices one year ahead during 2000 to 2012, it found that while the forecasts made by Hotelling's rule were, on average, the least biased, none of the methods were significantly better than the futures curve.[20]

Todays price as a predictor

Some research has gone even further and suggest that the best forecast is just today's price (in economics speak this is often known as "the Martingale model"). In 2007, economists Ron Alquist and Lutz Kilian published a paper in which they examined all the sophisticated methods one could use to determine the price of oil one month, one quarter or one year in the future.[21]

They looked at fancy econometric models, at oil prices in futures and spot markets and they also looked at the consensus opinion of oil analysts. They found that anyone could do better than all these crystal balls, sometimes far better, by simply applying a mindless rule: Always predict that the future price will be whatever the price is now. True, this technique is far from accurate, but the others are worse.

In late 2015, Alexandra Heath – the head of economic analysis at Australia's central bank, the Reserve Bank of Australia (RBA) – was questioned about how good the bank's track record at forecasting commodity prices was.[22] "Not very" was the answer. The RBA consistently under-appreciated the demand for commodities and, thus, the increase in Australia's terms of trade. Heath noted that:

> At the risk of oversimplifying, the task of forecasting the terms of trade for Australia is roughly equivalent to the task of forecasting commodity prices. A large part of the misses during the

> upswing of the terms of trade came down to an under-appreciation of how much demand for commodities would grow, and how long it would take for new supply to come to market. After a long period of low commodity prices, there wasn't sufficient production capacity to meet the increase in demand from China and other emerging markets. Prices increased, and there was a substantial increase in mining investment around the world in response.

In a telling remark that reflects much of the research documented in this chapter, she concludes with:

> ...at least in theory, spot financial prices should contain all the relevant information about supply and demand if these markets are reasonably deep and liquid. In this situation, it is difficult to do better than a "no-change" assumption for price projections.

Modelling ruptures in the trend

Having perfect foresight that prices will broadly go up or down in the future is useful, but it is not what investors, consumers and producers fear the most. For each of these actors in the market, it is the risk of extreme moves in prices, particularly against them, that keeps them awake at night. Unfortunately, all of the methods outlined above have little use in predicting abrupt changes in prices.

Models based on fundamentals rely on an assumption that commodity markets are linear. An increase in demand set against a fixed supply results in the price going up by some percentage. Commodity futures curves typically resemble smooth slopes stretching serenely far out into the future. Technical analysis, to its credit, can show when markets are vulnerable to sharp corrections, but even then only work by looking at set periods into the future based on patterns and other technical indicators. Technical analysis can't always tell you that something will happen, only that there is a risk of a certain price response if "it" happens. This point was picked up by Didier Sornette in his book "Why Stockmarkets Crash":[23]

> Predictions of trend reversals, changes of regime, or "ruptures" is extraordinarily difficult and unreliable in essentially all real-life domains of applications, such as economics, finance, weather, and climate. It is probably the most difficult challenge and arguably the most interesting and useful. The two known strategies for modeling, namely algebraic theories and brute-force numerical simulations of resulting large algebraic systems, are both unable to offer effective solutions for most concrete problems. Simulation studies of ruptures suffer from numerous sources of error, including model mispecifications [sic] and inaccurate numerical representation of the mathematical models, which are especially important for rare extreme events.

Sornette uses the example of how climate predictions have changed. In the 1970s, there was a growing consensus among scientists that the Earth was cooling down and there was concern we might enter a new ice age. In hindsight, we can see how short-sighted this prediction was, but it needed a century of data to see a clear signal. In climatology, the techniques available to scientists are bad at predicting most changes of regime. And economics is no different.

Let's focus on one of the main causes of abrupt changes in commodity price trends. Ruptures in the price trend for many commodities are often the result of geopolitical developments. Political scientists Ian Bremmer and Preston Keat defined geopolitics as: "The study of how geography, politics, strategy, and history combine to generate the rise and fall of great powers and wars among states." Given its importance to the running of the modern global economy, nowhere is this more vividly observed than in the battle for energy resources and, in particular, oil.

A cursory look at a simple oil price chart dating back to the 1970s reveals a series of bumps. Each of these bumps can be pinpointed to wars and conflicts, whether it was the Iranian revolution, the Iraqi invasion of Kuwait or the US-led invasion of Iraq. More recently, the Arab Spring-related uprisings in Libya or Egypt, civil war in Syria and violence in Iraq and the Ukraine have resulted in escalating geopolitical tensions across many important energy production and transit countries. There is a strong correlation between war casualties in energy producing countries and disruptions to oil output. As many historical episodes suggest, oil producing and distribution systems are hard to keep running when countries are immersed in civil wars or wars with neighbouring countries.

Other commodity markets also face their own geopolitical risk factors; the cocoa market, for example. Supply is concentrated in West

Africa and in one country in particular, the Ivory Coast (supplier of approximately 40% of the world's crop). Frequent political instability in the area has resulted in unrest and outright civil war, disrupting the production and export of cocoa from its ports.

If geopolitics plays such a big role in seismic moves in the oil market and many other commodities, then if geopolitical shifts can be forecasted with any accuracy this must give forecasters an edge, right? The Good Judgment Project, set up by Phillip Tetlock, set out to answer the first part of this question. They explored the profile of the best out of hundreds of forecasters who made over 150,000 predictions on roughly 200 events during a two year period. Forecasters were asked a multitude of questions, such as: Will the United Nations General Assembly recognise a Palestinian state by September 30th 2011? Will Bashar al-Assad remain president of Syria through to January 31st 2012? The researchers found that forecasters can be good at spotting changes, but only over long timescales.[24]

The problem with geopolitical events is that they tend to be binary outcomes (although clearly not always). They either happen in the future or they don't. This contrasts with what we might term "market" or "economic" risks which are more dynamic. There are three main problems with binary outcomes: first, they offer little information advantage for investors to play with; second, they are hard to predict and, third, they offer few easily identifiable markets that might benefit from a particular outcome.

Prediction markets have become popular as a way of bringing together disparate views on the outcome of a geopolitical event into one number – the odds of that event occurring within a particular time period. One now defunct prediction marketplace, InTrade, hosted several controversial geopolitical event markets. These included the date that Saddaam Hussein would be captured following the start of the Second Gulf War, when Osama bin Laden would be captured or killed and when Bashir Alisad, the President of Syria, would be deposed. More mundanely, and less controversial, prediction markets typically revolve around elections and referendums.

An election can pose a clear and obvious risk to investors, so information on it is likely to be highly sought after. Opinion polls are almost constantly being conducted, distributed and updated, at least in the major developed countries. Polling companies effectively run political polls as loss leaders – they serve as marketing for rest of their business. These polls are picked up by broadcasters and the media, hungry for information. So the dynamics of an election campaign mean that you are unlikely to ever gain any information advantage. If you believe you have an advantage, it is more likely to be the result of a gut feeling than of knowing something that others don't. Even if you gain some kind of information advantage through polling, you're relying on it to be correct – something far from certain.

The success of prediction markets, pre-Brexit and the 2016 US Presidential election, was extraordinary. Intrade and the Iowa Electronic Markets (the longest established online market, run by the University of Iowa) correctly called the winner of the Electoral College vote in all fifty states in the close 2004 election between George W. Bush and John Kerry. According to the University of Michigan economist Justin Wolfers, prediction markets perform better than the Gallup poll, which is much more expensive to compile. The average error on presidential elections (at least prior to 2016) for prediction markets is 1.4%; the equivalent number for Gallup is over 2%.[25]

As with commodity and other financial markets, betting markets are prone to bias too. Participants in the prediction markets for elections are unlikely to be representative of the people that actually vote – a possible reason why the markets failed to capture the possibility of the UK voting to leave the EU and Donald Trump winning the 2016 US Presidential election. Another problem with prediction markets is that they are not a voting machine, they are a weighing machine. Unlike a vote, your bet is worth more if you put more money behind it and that can create weaknesses. This includes the risk that other bettors just follow the money thinking it reflects fundamentals, but in doing so drive the price of an event away from the "fundamentals". There is also a risk that the market is manipulated to influence other, much larger financial markets (eg, currencies) that could be affected by the perception of one result or another occurring.

Even if you have fantastic foresight about how a geopolitical event is likely to develop, the next problem is decoding what the impact is likely to be on a range of different commodity markets. All too often pundits focus on the immediate effect; for example, based on whichever candidate wins an election. However, they forget to draw the dots as to how the "narrative" could change once the geopolitical uncertainty of the political event falls away.

Even if you could correctly forecast that the regime of a particular oil producing nation would be toppled within a given year, you wouldn't be able to know the exact path that oil prices would go as a result. You could at least add a risk premium to your forecast, but even that might not be correct and, as we discussed earlier, it is the risk of a sharp spike in prices that gets people's attention.

Although it may seem that economists, policymakers or financial market participants should be able to form accurate expectations about the future price of a commodity, this is not necessarily the case. The reason for this is that the price of a commodity will only be as predictable as its determinants, even if economic models of the global commodity market are approximately correct. Unless we can foresee the future evolution of these determinants, surprise changes in the price – that are driven by unexpected shifts in demand or supply – will be inevitable.[26]

Fancy economic models, futures curves, costs, technical analysis, political forecasting or exchange rates – whichever method you take, whichever combination you use, they will only work at anticipating future movements in commodity prices some of the time. No single approach works all of the time and the best commodity forecaster needs to know when to change their approach. Why are commodity prices so difficult to predict? That is the subject of the next chapter.

Chapter 4: The Economics of Commodities

"No matter how much research you do, you can neither predict nor control the future."

John Templeton

"Nobody has a clue," Jan Hatzius, Goldman Sachs' chief economist, said to Nate Silver in the book "The Signal and the Noise". "It's hugely difficult to forecast the business cycle. Understanding an organism as complex as the economy is very hard."[27]

According to Hatzius, forecasters face three fundamental challenges: first, it is very hard to determine cause and effect; second, that the economy is always changing and, third, that the data that they have to work with is pretty bad. Let's discuss each of these points in more detail.

Determining cause and effect

The conventional approach – advocated by university economics textbooks, enthralled by most economists and policymakers, and typical of much of the analysis that is devoted to commodity markets – is to just focus on demand and supply. Forecasters then assume that these values are known with confidence, with the interaction of demand and supply setting the equilibrium price. The reality, however, is different, and a lot more complicated. Both producers and consumers of oil and other commodities seek stability, yet experience and the theory of complex systems suggests that the commodity industry has never been in equilibrium.

Thinking of commodity markets as a system helps

explain other features. According to Melanie Mitchel, author of "*Complexity: A Guided Tour*", complex systems are "large networks of components with no central control and simple rules of operation that give rise to complex collective behavior, sophisticated information processing and adaptation". Mitchel offers real life examples of complex systems as diverse as ants, neurons and stockmarket traders. The activities of commodity futures traders are remarkably similar.[28]

Borrowing from the language of control engineering and population biology, systems can be analysed in terms of feedback loops; where an initial change or shock to the system results in a change in system outputs, which in turn influences the input conditions. Feedback loops make the analysis of commodity markets and the ability to forecast prices much more challenging. Traditional explanations for volatility focus on the low price-elasticity of supply and demand, long investment lead times and the backward-looking nature of price expectations. Complexity can also help explain some of the endemic instability in commodity markets.

Negative feedback mechanisms dampen the impact of an initial shock and are therefore stabilising, promoting a rapid return to the equilibrium. In contrast, positive feedback mechanisms exaggerate and amplify the impact of the initial shock and are therefore destabilising, delaying the return to the equilibrium. In the aftermath of a shock, positive feedback mechanisms may dominate, delaying the process of adjustment. Meanwhile, negative feedback mechanisms are more powerful later, promoting convergence to a new equilibrium.

The financier George Soros uses the term

"reflexivity" to describe this view of financial markets. According to Soros, market prices provide a distorted view of reality, but they can also affect the so-called fundamentals they are supposed to reflect:[29]

> I believe that market prices are always wrong in the sense that they present a biased view of the future. But distortion works in both directions: not only do market participants operate with a bias, but their bias can also influence the course of events. This may create the impression that markets anticipate future developments correctly, but in fact it is not present expectations that correspond to future events but future events that are shaped by present expectations. The participants' perceptions are inherently flawed, and there is a two-way connection between flawed perceptions and the actual course of events, which results in a lack of correspondence between the two. I call this two-way connection "reflexivity".

Reflexivity can set up a feedback loop between market valuations and the so-called fundamentals that are being valued, which can be either positive or negative:

> Negative feedback brings market prices and the underlying reality closer together. In other words, negative feedback is self-correcting. It can go on forever, and if the underlying reality remains unchanged, it may eventually lead to an equilibrium in which market prices accurately reflect the

fundamentals.

A positive feedback loop is self-reinforcing and can result in commodity prices rising to extreme highs or lows. But, as Soros goes onto say, even these have to return to Earth:

> It cannot go on forever because eventually, market prices would become so far removed from reality that market participants would have to recognize them as unrealistic. When that tipping point is reached, the process becomes self-reinforcing in the opposite direction. That is how financial markets produce boom-bust phenomena or bubbles. Bubbles are not the only manifestations of reflexivity, but they are the most spectacular.

Soros goes onto say that because financial markets, unlike natural science, have thinking participants "the symmetry between explanation and prediction that characterizes the laws of natural sciences is not attainable", and so "one can never be sure whether it is the expectation that corresponds to the subsequent event or the subsequent event that conforms to the expectation".

This reflexivity means that it is very difficult to say that a 5% increase in demand for oil next year will have this effect on prices. It's just not as deterministic as that and anyone that says it is needs to dig deeper. The way that market participants think about the future also affects the future: "When a situation has thinking participants, the sequence of events does not lead directly from one set of facts to the next; rather, it connects facts to perceptions and perceptions to facts in a shoelace pattern."

While events have impacts, the size of the impact does not correspond to the size of the initial event – so-called non-linear behaviour. Complex systems often exhibit non-linear behaviour in which small changes in initial conditions can generate large changes in outcomes. Non-linearity makes the behaviour of complex systems chaotic and hard to forecast over anything other than a short time horizon. French mathematician Henri Poincaré, the founder of dynamical systems theory, summed this up pretty well:

> If we knew exactly the laws of nature and the situation of the universe at the initial moment, we could predict exactly the situation of that same universe at a succeeding moment. But even if it were the case that the natural laws had no longer any secret for us, we could still only know the initial situation approximately. If that enabled us to predict the succeeding situation with the same approximation, that is all we require, and we should say that the phenomenon has been predicted, that it is governed by laws. But it is not always so; it may happen that small differences in the initial conditions produce very great ones in the final phenomenon. A small error in the former will produce an enormous error in the latter. Prediction becomes impossible...

Is there any evidence to support this view in commodity markets? A 2013 study by researchers at the United Nations Conference on Trade and Development (UNCTAD) and the Swiss Federal Institute of Technology examined price moves in Brent oil, US crude, soybeans, sugar, corn and wheat futures. They used an elaborate procedure designed to separate movements related to new information from those in which one price change begets another. They found that fundamental changes in supply and demand account for less than a third of short-term movements in commodity futures prices. Reflexive trading – when prices respond to past price changes rather than new information about fundamentals – accounts for 60-70% of price moves in the main commodity futures contracts, up from less than 40% before 2005. And although their study focused on short-term trading data, they found the existence of similar price dynamics over the longer term too.[30]

In layman's terms, the researchers have proved what traders have always instinctively understood: that prices are driven by a combination of fundamentals and behavioural factors, in proportions that vary over time.

When markets were in this state of high reflexivity, the "branching ratio" as the authors calculate it, was high. The branching ratio measures how much of the change in price is due to endogenous feedback processes (ie, past price movements) rather than exogenous news (ie, news that an oil pipeline had exploded). Looking at the price of crude oil, the authors found that the branching ratio was high in the run-up to the boom in oil prices in 2008 and stayed high on the way down as prices bottomed out in 2009. Beginning in 2011, the ratio spiked following the start of the Arab Spring and amid speculation that oil output from producers like Libya and Iraq could be disrupted.

As the report shows, perhaps the most remarkable result is that the ratio surged as oil prices rose towards a peak in 2008. The surge in prices during this time left many commentators suggesting that the oil price was a bubble. The uncertainty over the correct value of oil was amplified by data discrepancies between the International Energy Agency (IEA) and the US Energy Information Administration (EIA). This meant that market analysts could not decide whether excess demand or supply shortages had caused the rise in oil prices. Remember, the more imprecise the estimate of the fundamental value of an asset, the more room there is for a convincing narrative – aka "stories" that can justify speculative bubble prices.

The strength, timing and co-integration of all these feedback loops are the challenges that commodity price forecasters face. Therefore, the first implication from the complexity theory in markets is that try as commodity forecasters might to understand the future by looking at back to a similar set of circumstances in the past, the sensitive dependence on initial conditions means that in chaotic and complex systems even the tiniest errors in initial measurements will produce large errors in the forecasts of future prices.

Following on from this, another important implication from complexity theory in relation to markets is that even if the initial conditions are comparable, it doesn't follow that the resulting events will work out the same. Reflexivity in commodity markets means that the factors that influence prices now may not be the same factors that influence prices tomorrow. The impact that market participants' expectations have on fundamentals changes, and those same participants' reaction to market fundamentals, and the actions of other participants, will evolve.

The documented high levels of reflexivity are likely to make the price formation process less efficient. This is because higher reflexivity implies a slower convergence towards a fundamental (equilibrium) value. High levels of reflexivity imply the existence of a large susceptibility of the system regarding external shocks. When the price discovery process is dominated by internal feedback mechanisms, even a small initial shock to the system may turn into a large crash or spike in prices.

The accuracy of forecasting the weather fades as the forecast horizon lengthens because it's impossible to forecast the complex interactions. We put little faith in weather forecasts suggesting that there will be a "barbecue summer", so why do we put faith in forecasts that commodity prices will do this or that over the next year?

Let's look at the oil market as an example.

According to economist Paul Frankel, "There is always too much or too little oil". Since the oil market has a tendency to move from one extreme to another, crises almost inevitably follow since neither production or consumption are self-adjusting. Frankel blamed the lack of smooth adjustment on the limited responsiveness of supply and demand to moderate changes in prices, at least in the short run. Frankel's words, published just after the end of World War Two, are a perfect description of the subsequent boom and bust in oil during the 1970s and early 1980s, and again between 2004 and 2016.[31]

Both producers and consumers of oil and other commodities also seek stability, yet experience and the theory of complex systems suggests that the commodity industry has never been in equilibrium. Commodity markets are in a perpetual state of disequilibrium; at any point they may move further away from equilibrium rather than towards it. The process is complicated because there is not just one "oil market". Instead there are a series of separate but related markets for crude, fuels, refining, oilfield services, engineering construction, drilling equipment, skilled labour and raw materials, etc. Each of these markets are subject to their own feedback mechanisms and operate at different speeds, the balance of which is constantly changing.

An example of a negative feedback loop in the oil and energy markets is consumers switching to cheaper, alternative fuels to save money after a rise in the price of oil. Another example is fuel efficiency, whereby car manufacturers invest in producing more fuel-efficient engines. Meanwhile, as oil prices rise, higher revenues in oil producing countries will be circulated back into US assets, like the Treasury market (so-called Petrodollars). In turn, this will push up the value of the US dollar, making oil more expensive in dollar terms. A final example of a negative feedback loop, this time one that influences the supply of oil, is finance. Investors will seek to direct the funds they manage to where the return is greatest. If the price of oil has gone up, and investors at least expect the increase to be maintained, then they will want to move funds to take advantage of higher future revenue streams.

An example of a positive feedback loop again includes the impact on the economies of oil producing countries. Higher oil revenues will encourage greater spending by their governments, which will then feed through into more consumer and infrastructure spending and in turn increase the demand for oil. On the supply side, service contracts between the oil producer and the many number of subsidiaries they use (eg, rig suppliers, maintenance contracts and shipping) means that supply can't just be halted on the basis of a whim. Instead, supply may have to be adjusted with a time lag to take account of the oil producers' contract commitments.

Just as its very difficult to determine cause and effect in the past, it's even harder to do it in the near future, even when you have a good grasp of all the information that could affect prices. In the first two months after Iraq invaded Kuwait in 1992, the oil price doubled from around $20 per barrel to almost $40 per barrel. If you asked any intelligent "analyst" or journalist he would have predicted a rise in the price of oil in the event of war. Their reasoning would have been simple – war in the most important oil producing region in the world creates the risk of disruption to oil distribution and supply.

In 1992, oil prices rose relentlessly as the war drums were beating louder and louder in Kuwait, until the cacophony became unbearable. As soon as it became likely that the US and its allies would invade Kuwait to push back the invading Iraqi forces, oil prices gradually fell back. Indeed, once the US-led coalition began its bombing campaign, in a matter of days prices fell from $30 per barrel to below $20 per barrel. As Nassim Taleb's fictional character, Tony, describes in the book "Fooled by Randomness", "War could cause a rise in oil prices, but not scheduled war – since prices adjust to expectations. It has to be in the price."[32]

It is tempting to prescribe economic rationality to why prices have done this or that in the past. However, market expectations can have an out-sized influence on the connection between an event and the subsequent impact on price. Often it can be the uncertainty relating to an event that drives prices higher, but then prices fall back once the "event" has occurred and the uncertainty has diminished.

The economy is always changing

Economies are subject to both cyclical and structural changes. Examples of cyclical changes include the short-term business cycle, longer-term commodity and currency cycles and of course the political cycle driven by periodic elections. Meanwhile, structural factors typically include factors like technological change that affect long-term productivity and economic growth.

Different stages of the business cycle have different characteristics. According to the National Bureau of Economic Research (NBER), there have been 11 business cycles in the US from 1945 to 2009, with the average length of a cycle lasting a little less than six years. Of course, the average disguises a wide variation, and there is some evidence to suggest that recent business cycles have lengthened. At the end of a typical business cycle, inflation tends to increase as economies near full employment and cost pressures feed through the economy. Meanwhile, forward-looking investors in commodities know that this period tends to be favourable to commodity prices and so they invest, in anticipation of the higher inflation.

Commodities have much larger cycles too driven by both fundamental and financial factors. Research examining centuries of commodity price data has sketched a pattern of 15-20 year super-cycles (a period of rising prices), followed by a slide in prices over the following 10-15 years. At any period in the cycle, a shock to supply or demand will have a very different impact on the price. When the market for a particular commodity is tight (say supply is thought to be constrained by the weather or a geopolitical risk), prices are likely to react much faster and more violently than when supply is thought to be ample (such as when there is large stock availability in relation to consumption). The US dollar also goes through cycles driven by the business cycle and interest rate differentials. Since most commodities are also priced in US dollars, a weakening in the currency also acts to support commodity prices.

Also implicit in any economic forecast (and in many commodity forecasts) is an understanding of how policy decisions may affect commodity prices. For example, how will higher economic growth affect the US Federal Reserve's future decisions over interest rates? Forecasts also need to into take account how commodity prices may influence the policy decisions of commodity producers; for example, the response of the Organisation of Petroleum Exporting Countries (OPEC) to low oil prices, or what the government of a commodity exporting nation will do to respond to poor export revenue.

Much more significant when considering the long-term outlook for prices are structural factors. Implicit in any forecast of commodity prices is an assumption of how technology could evolve and how its adoption will affect commodity prices. Commodity prices provide the incentive for new technology, yet also influence commodity production and consumption. Innovations, once introduced, may lead to higher yields from agriculture, more oil being extracted from offshore wells and deeper mines to extract more metals and minerals – all of which could eventually lead to rising commodity supplies.

High commodity prices may also lead to innovation on the demand side too. High energy prices, for example, may discourage consumers from using a particular energy inefficient product. This acts as an incentive for companies to redesign their products to become more energy efficient and less resource intensive. However, just because a technology might appear to be negative for demand doesn't mean it has to be bad for prices, at least not in the short to medium term. For example, if oil producers are worried about the growth in electric vehicles they may decide to postpone large scale, multi-decade, multi-billion dollar investments. If they get it wrong and electric vehicles don't take off as fast as they expect, then oil prices may rise sharply if there isn't enough supply to meet demand.

And remember, don't forget about rebound effects. If an innovation results in a energy intensive product (transportation for example) becoming cheaper or more accessible consumers are likely to want to consume more of it. Every improvement in technology has a rebound effect.

It's the uncertainty over how current technology can be utilised and how technology could evolve that makes forecasting so difficult. Technological developments of all sorts involve a large dose of serendipity. The philosopher Karl Popper perhaps best describes the struggle to anticipate future innovations: "The course of human history is strongly influenced by the growth of human knowledge." Popper also wrote:

> But it's impossible to "predict", by rational or scientific methods, the future growth of our scientific knowledge because doing so would require us to know that future knowledge and, if we did, it would

be present knowledge, not future knowledge.

Yet to forecast the price of oil, lead or cobalt into the next decade we need to make some assumption about how technology will make it easier to extract these commodities and how technology will change the demand for these commodities. Note that no one predicted the invention of pig iron or imagined how it would affect the nickel market, neither did anyone anticipate the introduction of hydraulic fracking and how it would turn the market for oil on its head.

Poor data quality

Basic statistics and forecasts about oil reserves, production, consumption and stocks ought to be a matter of routine. You stick a gauge at the end of a pipe and measure the amount of liquid flowing through, right? However, it's not that simple, and the problem isn't limited to just oil, but to all commodities.

Doubts about the reliability of energy statistics were a major part of the "energy crisis" that erupted during the 1970s. As late as 1968, the US reportedly had four million barrels per day of spare production capacity. Meanwhile, thousands of wells across Texas and Louisiana were being operated for fewer than ten days per month. But by March 1972, spare capacity had dropped to zero; every well was at maximum production, domestic output was falling and politicians spoke of an energy crisis.

The oil embargo, announced in October 1973, intensified the sense that something had gone badly wrong, leaving the US unprepared. Politicians and the media blamed a conspiracy between domestic producers and OPEC for engineering the crisis to drive up prices and profits. Congress held hearings amid a sense the statistics and forecasts prepared by oil and gas producers and the US Department of the Interior had been inaccurate or manipulated. One outcome of the crisis was the creation of a new US Department of Energy, and within it a new Energy Information Administration (EIA), in 1977, to produce more accurate and independent data. Another was the creation of the International Energy Agency (IEA) in 1974, to gather better statistics and bring greater transparency to the international energy markets.

Improvements in data collection and forecasting in the US, led by the EIA, have by and large quelled controversy about domestic US oil production, consumption and stocks; but that doesn't mean they are free from error or revision. According to a study by the *Wall Street Journal* (WSJ), annual estimates of global crude demand by the IEA in the seven years until 2016 were underestimated by an average of 880,000 barrels per day. And there is little evidence that the demand forecasts from others are any more accurate. The EIA also underestimated global demand - by an average of 2.3 million barrels a day.[33]

Demand is much harder to estimate than supply. Unlike supply, which can be estimated from the pre-announced expansion plans of a relatively small number of companies, estimating demand involves billions of consumers worldwide and many millions of companies of all sizes.

Revisions to oil supply estimates are typically much smaller than for demand, and are often about correcting overestimates for crude production. The IEA's supply data has been revised down 60,000 barrels a day on average over the seven years to 2016, according to the

WSJ's analysis. That means the oversupply usually ends up being smaller than initially thought. The history of data discrepancies underscores how oil markets often trade on incomplete data.

The information collected in many other parts of the world remains much less comprehensive and accurate. Two major sources of uncertainty are the deliberate secrecy of the major oil producing countries and poor data collection in emerging markets.

In late 2016, OPEC producer Iraq published an unprecedented level of detail about its oil producing activities. Instead of providing just one figure for output and one figure for how much it was exporting, the Iraqi authorities released detailed data about the crude oil output at each of its 26 oilfields and detailed export figures. This "transparency" was a calculated move to prove to outside observers, and other OPEC members in particular, that secondary source estimates of its oil production were way too high. In doing so, it was also making the case that Iraq should not be subject to output cuts.[34]

The opaqueness of oil data from OPEC producers is nothing new. As with any oligopolistic organisation, there is an incentive for individual OPEC members to misinform. This can take the form of underreporting the amount they are producing and the size of their reserves, but it can also result in outright disregard for pre-agreed production cuts – the higher the price of oil, the greater the incentive for an individual member to break the agreement. Remember, each OPEC member is a sovereign country, meaning that they are not legally obliged to commit to or honour any agreement.

The oil market is by far the largest, most

liquid and most important commodity market in the world. If such big revisions are made in the oil market, then imagine how difficult it becomes to estimate demand and supply and then forecast prices in much smaller markets such as lead, live cattle or lithium.

Opaqueness can also be a feature of major commodity consumers too. Despite China's undoubted influence on global commodity markets, developments in its economy continue to remain opaque and hence so too are its implications for commodity prices. Unreliable data makes it difficult to assess risk, which raises the probability of some internal shock. Statistics are never completely accurate, especially when trying to estimate activity in far flung parts of the world. An analyst trying to figure out where the price of copper is going next has to first look at what could happen to copper demand growth. Will it slow, increase or even fall? For this you need to look at what businesses consume lots of copper, not just in the US, Europe or China but also in emerging economies where the quality and frequency of data may leave much to be desired.

Even if there were copious amounts of statistics available in real time and covering all aspects of demand and supply, that doesn't mean that the data is the best and the final estimate. Think about population growth for a minute, which is thought by many to be the most predictable of all variables that could affect future demand for commodities. Ignoring the uncertainty about the future, even the baseline from which you could take a forecast is uncertain and subject to frequent revisions. As Dan Gardener remarks in his book "Future Babble":[35]

>...demographic facts like this are based on available research, and

when new research suggests the established "fact" isn't accurate, it has to be changed. Between 1951 and 1966, the official estimate of the world's population in 1951 changed 17 times.

Uncertainty about what is happening to commodity supply and demand, and thus the overall commodity balance, is not without cost. The uncertainty is likely to increase the risk premium that commodity producers use to decide on whether to invest or not. This increases the cost of that investment, perhaps resulting in delays or cancellations. The cost of which will only be felt during the next upturn in commodity prices when, yet again, producers may be caught in the dark.

Chapter 5: The Stories we Tell

"Those who have knowledge don't predict. Those who predict don't have knowledge."

Lao Tzu, sixth century BC poet

The Canadian economist Jeff Rubin had a good record of forecasting oil prices. In 2000, Rubin correctly predicted oil would top $50 per barrel by 2005. In 2005 he got it right again, forecasting prices would top $100 per barrel in 2007. In the first half of 2008, Rubin saw oil prices going nowhere but up. "Don't think of today's prices as a spike," he told the *Toronto Star*. "Don't think of them as a temporary aberration. Think of them as the beginning of a new era."

Nine months later, the price of oil crashed.

In 2009 and 2010, Rubin was quoted in countless stories about oil prices; the stories routinely noted Rubin's "oracular reputation", as *Newsweek* put it. Rubin "accurately predicted oil's surge during the last decade", wrote *Business Week*. He has been "deadly accurate", reported the *National Post*. All of these statements are true, but what none of these stories mention is that he missed calling the dramatic fall in the price of oil in 2008. Therefore, undeterred by his 2008 miss, Rubin, the former Chief Economist of CIBC World Markets, became even more bullish. In his 2009 book "Why Your World is About to Get a Whole Lot Smaller", he predicted that a barrel of oil would cost $225 per barrle by 2012.[36]

The 24 hour news cycle loves a pundit. They appear from out of nowhere to regurgitate the very same view they made just a few weeks ago. What the financial media never does is ask them "You were on air with us six months ago and you said oil would double in price. It's now halved. What went wrong?" The pundit is the worst kind of forecaster – never, ever held to account, but in the strongest position of all to influence the minds of investors.

In 1985, Philip Tetlock, a psychologist from the University of Pennsylvania, invited 284 experts to assign probabilities that particular well-defined events would occur in the not too distant future. All were acknowledged experts in their fields, with more than half holding PhDs. A few years later, when comparing the predictions with what actually happened, Tetlock found that the predictions made by these experts were better than those of a group of undergraduates, but not by much. As Tetlock put it: "We reach the point of diminishing marginal predictive returns for knowledge disconcertingly quickly." Tetlock also said: "Ironically, the more famous the expert, the less accurate his or her predictions tend to be."

It is those thinkers who are most renowned for their expertise in forecasting, whether it is commodity prices or anything else, who have the most to lose from mistakes. The most influential people have the greatest incentive to reframe the evidence to support their initial conclusions. The confidence of the pundit can be infectious though. The only rational way that consumers of forecasts can judge whether a pundit is likely to be right, at least to the casual and time-pressed observer, is how confident the forecaster appears to be.

Confidence is a good thing if the track record of the forecaster rises – he or she can then be expected to feel more confident that their subsequent predictions will also turn out well. There are two problems with this, however:

first, confidence can quickly turn to overconfidence and second, as con-men have known since the beginning of time, the appearance of confidence can be used to take advantage of people.

The Dunning-Kruger effect asserts that the ignorant (or incompetent) are unable to appreciate how ignorant (incompetent) they are. Bad drivers think they are good drivers. People who flunked a test often believe they did okay on it. Those lacking a sense of humour think they know what is funny. In comparison, people who are actually good at these things have a much more realistic assessment of their skills. Psychologists David Dunning and Justin Kruger, and their colleagues, established that this applies in a wide variety of contexts.[37]

There is also a lot of evidence that despite many types of experts and forecasters having little predictive power, they have plenty of confidence. This list of professions doesn't just include psychics and astrologers, but also credentialed economic forecasters, political pundits and active money managers. These experts may try to predict something that isn't very predictable, at least not by any known means. These experts are smart yet "incompetent" at what they do, thus making them subject to Dunning-Kruger psychology – they believe they are better forecasters than they actually are.

Psychologists Joseph R. Radzevick and Don A. Moore tested this dynamic with an experiment in which people were assigned either the role of "guesser" or "adviser". The job of guessers was to estimate the weight of people in photos; the more accurate they were, the more money they made. As well as providing weight estimates, the guessers also had to indicate the confidence they had in their accuracy. The guessers were free to choose any adviser's estimate, so advisers were also able make money based on the number of guessers who took their advice. Not surprisingly, the advisers were over-confident in the first rounds of the experiment. Advisers weren't punished for being inaccurate. In fact, guessers preferred the more confident advisers, and the advisers responded by getting more confident as the experiment progressed - even though their accuracy never improved.[38]

Competition between forecasters for clients or to appear on the 24 hour business news cycle may magnify over-confidence, ultimately reducing the value those consuming those forecasts may see. Financial TV provides the perfect platform for purveyors of ill-thought out forecasts from fame hungry pundits eager to pedal their wares. But remember, financial TV is designed for entertainment - not to make you better at making the right financial decisions. Like any form of entertainment, financial TV is designed as an assault on your senses, with all manner of irrelevant information. This is made worse because financial TV enshrines forecasts and those providing them front and centre.

According to Tetlock pundits typically fall into categories - "foxes" and "hedgehogs". Foxes pursue many different ends, often unrelated and even contradictory; they entertain ideas using divergent thinking (ie, looking at many possible outcomes), rather than convergent thinking, and they also don't seek to fit these ideas into, or exclude them from, any one all-embracing inner vision.

However, many of the pundits courting the financial limelight are hedgehogs. You can easily spot a hedgehog - they are characterised by an attitude of relating everything back to a single vision, and they over simplify and come across as much more confident in their outlook on the world in order to produce a compelling narrative. Terry Pratchett captures this flaw in human nature perfectly in his novel "The Truth":[39]

> Be careful. People like to be told what they already know. Remember that. They get uncomfortable when you tell them new things. New things...well, new things aren't what they expect. They like to know that, say, a dog will bite a man. That is what dogs do. They don't want to know that man bites a dog, because the world is not supposed to happen like that. In short, what people think they want is news, but what they really crave is olds...Not news but olds, telling people that what they think they already know is true.

We, as investors and business people, like the story – the narrative explaining how the future will turn out – to put structure to the apparent uncertainty and volatility going on in the world. We like stories, we like to summarise, we like to be able to reduce a complex interaction of multiple factors into a single sentence sound bite; for example: "lower, for longer" and "the cure for high prices, is high prices". As Nicholas Taleb points out, this fallacy "distorts our mental representation of the world; it is particularly acute when it comes to the rare event."[40]

According to the great English poet and philosopher Samuel Taylor Coleridge (1772-1834), enjoyment of fiction requires a "willing suspension of disbelief" — a conscious decision. But as Jonathan Gottschall, author of "The Storytelling Animal: How Stories Make Us

Human" explains, that's not how it works in practice:[41]

> We don't *will* our suspension of disbelief. If the story is strong, if the teller has craft, our suspension of disbelief *happens to us*, with or without our permission. Chalk it up to the power of emotion. Successful stories generate powerful feelings, and strong feelings act as a solvent on our logic and our skepticism. To put it positively, good stories—fictional or not—make us more open minded. To put it negatively, they make us a lot more gullible.

Lack of information creates a vacuum for stories to breed, an environment in which a compelling narrative can capture the imagination. The more imprecise the estimate of the fundamental value of an asset, the more room there is for "stories" and "new economy" thinking to justify speculative prices. This same need for information redux is what pundits of all shapes feed on, whether in commodity markets or anywhere else.

In the "rational" view of the world, investors and decision makers first observe the evidence, then weigh the evidence and finally come to a decision. In the rational view, we all collect the evidence in a well-behaved and unbiased fashion. The reality, however, is that we are prone to only look for the information which agrees with our prior view (confirmatory bias, etc). The second stage of the rational decision is a weighing of the evidence. However, a more commonly encountered approach is to construct a narrative to explain the evidence that has been gathered (the story model of thinking). We humans are, by our deepest natures, suckers for a story.

A credible narrative can help make the case for commodities and other assets too. Investment banks, journalists and others will produce "theme" reports that pose a question or a statement relating to where the next opportunity might come from. Many of these reports are produced for entertainment, but also to infuse clients with a sense that they have been given access to superior insight that will enable them to be (or at least to feel that they are) one step ahead of the rest of the herd.

Narrative economics

Economists, financial market pundits and forecasters often think they are just observers of the facts. Most, I presume, would regard the assumption that the way they think about the world can also change it as being fanciful. Yet it only takes a bit of reflection to see that a lot of economics concerns self-fulfilling (or self-averting) phenomena. An economy can go into recession when enough people think it will, for instance. Therefore, forecasters of all stripes have a responsibility.

Robert Shiller suggests that economics should be expanded to include the serious quantitative study of changing popular narratives in causing fluctuations in economic activity. As Shiller shows, the economics profession has had little to say about the role of narratives compared with other social sciences; something I hope to address through this book.[42]

According to Shiller:

> [The] human brain has always been highly tuned towards narratives, whether factual or not, to justify

ongoing actions, even such basic actions as spending and investing. Stories motivate and connect activities to deeply felt values and needs. Narratives "go viral" and spread far, even worldwide, with economic impact.

Are narratives becoming increasingly based on false ideas or, at least, "alternative truths"? In an information vacuum, such as that which exists in commodity markets, then this is possible. According to Shiller, "A phishing equilibrium with a certain equilibrium acceptable level of dishonesty in narrative is established." Hardly encouraging!

The 2016 US Presidential Election brought considerable attention to the phenomenon of "fake news": entirely fabricated and often highly partisan content that is presented as factual news. Of course, disinformation of this sort poses a major threat to democracy, but it also poses a threat to the ability of investors in all financial assets to gauge new information and analysis accurately. Research at Yale University by Gordon Pennycock, Tyrone D. Cannon and David G. Rand found that familiarity increases the perceived accuracy of statements, whether they are true or false, or plausible or implausible. Using actual fake news headlines presented as they are seen on Facebook, the researchers showed that even a single exposure increases perceptions of accuracy. Given the ease with which "convincing narratives" can be created and distributed on social media platforms, combined with our increasing tendency to consume financial market news via social media, it is likely that we are being exposed to fake and potentially misleading stories with much greater frequency than in the past.[43]

False trends arise when a narrative is founded on untrue assumptions, but the narrative is so strong it moves price action anyway. Then, as prices rise, it confirms the narrative in the minds of investors, which in turn reinforces the view they should buy into the increase in prices. A compelling narrative that is not balanced by credible evidence can have harmful effects much wider than just a handful of investors losing money. It can mean the loss of community's livelihoods, affecting entire economies and wasting valuable resources – financial, social and environmental. In the wrong hands, narratives can spread like wildflowers.

Cult followings

I will not disparage anyone's personal beliefs; they are entitled to them. But, this does not mean you need to fall sucker to those beliefs. Some investments can literally take on a cult following lasting for months, years or several decades or more. Outside of commodity markets think of Warren Buffet (whose disciples have followed him for decades), technology stocks or Bitcoin. The latter, it could be argued is a perfect example of a "belief" in a system that resonates with a person's inner beliefs about liberty and technology.

My point in connecting "beliefs" with commodity market forecasts is that "beliefs" can often be expressed very passionately by pundits, whether on TV or in an article, but often the reasons why he or she could be wrong are not considered. This is something to be very wary of. A form of closed-loop thinking can develop, where failure denial can become so deeply entrenched in investors' minds and systems, in which any reasoned argument of the pros and cons becomes impossible. Any reversal of the desired price trend is seen not as a reason to question the investment hypothesis, but as a sign of non-believers selling out and so an opportunity for the believer to raise the stakes.

An example from suburban Michigan makes this clear. In his seminal book "When Prophecy Fails", Leon Festinger, one of the most influential sociologists of the last half century, tells the true story of a housewife called Marian Keech. Marian claimed to be in psychic contact with a god-like figure from another planet. This deity had told her that a gigantic flood would cause the world to end before dawn on 21st December 1954. Keech warned her friends about the impending disaster. Some left their jobs and homes, despite resistance from their families, to move in with the woman who had by now become their spiritual leader. They were told that true believers would be saved by a spaceship that would swoop down and pick them up from Keech's garden at midnight.[44] [45]

Festinger was fascinated by how the group would react after the prophecy failed – surely they would just return to their old lives and denounce Keech as a fraud for lulling them into selling up? As such, Festinger and his colleagues infiltrated the group and gained their trust. They sat in Keech's house so that they could observe the trust of her believers in the so-called psychic. As the deadline for the apocalypse passed, with no sign of a spaceship (and still less a flood), Festinger and his colleagues watched the reactions of the cult members. At first, they kept checking outside to see if the spaceship had landed and then, as the clock ticked further past midnight, they became sullen and bemused.

Soon a strange thing happened. The faith of the hardcore members became defiant. Faced with what should have been crushing disappointment, their faith seemed to strengthen. Instead of acknowledging that the prediction had failed, they redefined the failure. As Festinger put it: "The little group, sitting all night long, had spread so much light that God had saved the world from destruction." They were "jubilant".

While these behaviours are extreme, they provide an insight into psychological mechanisms that are universal. When we are confronted with evidence that challenges our deeply held beliefs, we are more likely to reframe the evidence than we are to alter our beliefs. We invent new reasons, new justifications and new explanations. Sometimes we just ignore the evidence altogether. The same can be said for those beliefs (whether instructed by hope or fear) represented in forecasts of future commodity prices – first geopolitical breakdown, then the collapse of the current monetary system, then inflation rearing its head, then population running out of control, then..., then... and so on and so on.

Just as it's important not to become wedded to a financial position, it's important not to become too attached to a story. When an investment thesis only includes the factors that could move a market in one direction, but includes nothing to caveat that or to draw attention to why the forecast might be wrong, you know something is amiss. This is where you need to ask yourself and the commodity forecaster more and better questions. Understand that the world is dynamic and that even if there is a strong theme that appears to mean prices can only go one way, there will be a countervailing force that will slow or cause a reversal in the market.

Most stories at least begin with some element of truth, but they don't always end that way.

So what are some of the main commodity market stories that have had a powerful influence over investors, governments and entire industries and economies? In the next part of this chapter, I outline some of the main longer-term (often very longer-term) themes that have captured investor attention.

Population explosion

Thomas Robert Malthus was a British cleric and scholar. His principle work, "An Essay on the Principle of Population" published in 1798, suggested that although populations rise exponentially, agricultural output could only increase arithmetically because of the finite amount of land available. As a result, "positive checks" (described by Malthus as higher mortality caused by famine, disease and war) were necessary to bring the number of people back in line with the capacity to feed them. How very depressing!

In the second edition, published in 1803, Malthus softened his original harsh message by introducing the idea of moral restraint. Such a "preventive check", operating through the birth rather than the death rate, could provide a way to counter the otherwise inexorable logic of too many mouths chasing too little food. If couples had fewer children, the population growth could be slowed for agriculture to cope.

The basic tenets of Malthus' theory have, until now at least, proven false, because what he didn't count on was human ingenuity. Since the 1800s, dramatic improvements in agricultural productivity, the expansion of international trade, and legislative reform have resulted in vast increases in food production and lower prices. In turn, this has enabled a much larger population to be supported.

Looking back over several centuries of food prices, the data suggests that Malthus was onto something. Wheat prices in the UK rose more than four-fold in real terms between 1550 and 1800, so you can at least understand why he was concerned. Like many pundits, Malthus' timing was terrible. In the early nineteenth century, shortly after he published his research, wheat prices began a long and inexorable decline.[46]

More recently, the book "The Limits to Growth", commissioned by The Club of Rome, was published in 1972. In a similar vein to Malthus, the book states that if the Earth's consumption patterns and population growth continued, then it would hit its limit within a century. What later became known as the Malthusian Catastrophe continues to be popular to this day. The recent food price hikes of 2008-2011 have reinvigorated proponents of Malthus' theories, that the world is facing a much more difficult future, one that may check population growth.

Paul Ehrlich (ecologist, doomsayer and author of the 1968 book "The Population Bomb") also thought that overpopulation would cause disaster and widespread scarcity. Paul Ehrlich's bleak vision in "The Population Bomb" was anything but that of a lone crank. Countless experts made similar forecasts in the 1950s and 1960s. In his book, Ehrlich declared, "the battle to feed all of humanity is over. In the 1970s, the world will undergo famines – hundreds of millions of people will starve to death in spite of any crash programs embarked upon now." But there weren't mass famines in the 1970s, or in the 1980s. Thanks to the dramatic improvements in agriculture collectively known as "the Green Revolution" (which were well underway by the time Ehrlich wrote his book), food production not only kept up with population growth, it greatly surpassed it. Between 1961 and 2000, the world's population doubled and the calories of food consumed per person increased 24%. Ehrlich said it was impossible.

Even today, many people still insist that Paul Ehrlich was essentially on the mark in "The Population Bomb". One of those people is Paul Ehrlich himself! In a 2009 essay, Ehrlich acknowledged that the book "underestimated the impact of the Green Revolution" and so the starvation he expected wasn't as bad as he predicted. However, he insisted that the book's grim vision was accurate, stating that its "most serious flaw" was that it was "much too optimistic about the future".

The economist Julian Simon, meanwhile, suggested people would find substitutes for scarce resources and that everything would turn out fine. To resolve their dispute, the two men agreed to have a bet on the price of commodities. Ehrlich agreed to buy $1,000 worth of five key metals – copper, tin, chrome, nickel and tungsten – in 1980. They would be sold in 1990. If the sale price, in 1980 dollars, were higher, then Ehrlich would win and reap the profit. If the proceeds were lower, Simon would win and Ehrlich would pay him the difference. Ten years passed and the metals were worth considerably less in 1990 than they had been in 1980, Simon won. Ehrlich sent a cheque to his rival.

Simon was lucky with his bet. The spike in oil prices in the late 1970s was one factor that contributed to the slowing in industrial growth in the 1980s, which in turn resulted in lower prices for the five metals. As the maxim goes, "The cure for high prices, is high prices". Simon was also lucky with his timing, if the bet had taken place twenty years later, starting in the year 2000, things would have turned out very different.

Simon was so confident in his lower for longer prognosis for commodity prices that in the two editions of his book "The Ultimate Resource", published in 1981 and 1996, he wrote the following:[47]

> This is a public offer to stake $10,000, in separate transactions of $1,000 or $100 each, on my belief that mineral resources (or food or other commodities) will not rise in price in future years, adjusted for inflation. You choose any mineral or other raw material (including grain and fossil fuels) that is not government controlled, and the date of settlement.

Both men, Ehrlich and Simon, were bad at making predictions – the economist and the environmentalist – but both were equally good at raising their profiles as pundits.

Drowning in oil

In what is now one of the magazine's most infamous articles, *The Economist* published a report in March 2009 highlighting how the price of oil had fallen to just over $10 per barrel to its lowest level in real terms since 1973. The article postulated whether given the trend in prices since the late 1900s that prices could, and should, fall even further:[48]

> Yet here is a thought: $10 might actually be too optimistic. We may be heading for $5... Thanks to new technology and productivity gains, you might expect the price of oil, like that of most other commodities, to fall slowly over the years. Judging by the oil market in the pre-OPEC era, a "normal" market

> price might now be in the $5-10 range. Factor in the current slow growth of the world economy and the normal price drops to the bottom of that range.

The magazine goes on to list several trends, extrapolations from recent events, that justify prices falling even further. The article cites low production costs in the Middle East and elsewhere as evidence that even if the price of oil rebounded, those low cost producers would quickly raise output in response. It also cites emerging worries over global warming for why oil demand could be lower in the future as countries looked to meet binding emissions targets. Finally, the article also argues that low oil prices would not provide much of a boost to consumption; partly due to new energy technologies and partly due to environmental taxes disguising low oil prices from consumers. No mention was made of China, India or the rise of other emerging economies that were to power the rise in oil consumption over the next 10-15 years.

To give them some credit however, and in a prescient move, *The Economist* highlighted a risk that was to become important four years later:

> In the medium term, however, the Gulf states will find that their revenues recover and even increase with cheaper oil. So once they have made the transition to higher production, a $5 world should not hold any terrors for them. But it may hold more terrors for the rest of the world—for, just as in 1973, it will find that it is increasingly dependent on a few unstable and unreliable Gulf countries, notably

Saudi Arabia, Iran and Iraq, for its energy. Cheap oil may not look quite so wonderful, after all.

As with high prices, so it is with low prices, we often adjust our story and our view of the world to fit the price. Human nature is equally prone to construct a narrative as to why prices may stay lower for longer – a narrative that can also be as misinformed as peak oil and just as damaging.

BRICs

"Another day, another record high in commodity prices," wrote Goldman Sachs' analysts in a May 2006 report in which they said the BRICs – Brazil, Russia, India and China – would continue to fuel demand for a wide range of commodities. The handy acronym BRIC made its debut in a 2001 report by Goldman Sachs economist Jim O'Neill, when the four nations it referred to made up approximately 8% of the world's total economy. For more than a decade later, the theory that Brazil, Russia, India, China (and later South Africa) should be treated as a linked economic force representing the rise of emerging markets drove everything from the creation of new financial institutions to billions of dollars in investment decisions from fund managers and consumer companies. It was also a compelling reason for commodity prices to rise sharply higher.

The early 2000s was marked with an obsession with China. Investors piled into commodities on the basis that China was the largest consumer of almost everything. Many observed the rise of the BRICs and saw Malthus' fears resurface – so many new people, with so many demands on food, energy and consumer goods, must inevitably upend the global supply of resources. However, commodity market pundits make a mistake when they focus too much on the supply/demand issues of today without either looking back at historical patterns or out into the future.

To his credit, Jim O'Neil did not shy away from stating that the growth of the BRICs did not mean that commodity prices would rise forever. In his 2011 book "The Growth Map", he noted that, "Oil prices are affected, of course, by supply and demand, but they also themselves affect supply and demand. The more oil costs, the fewer people want to heat their houses with it, or use it to get to work." O'Neil goes onto say that, "I have heard it argued that the pressure on resource prices and availability will persist regardless of what happens in China and India. I find this difficult to believe." But, perhaps, the seed was already sown in the minds of investors, company executives and commodity forecasters that prices would continue to rise.[49]

Back in 2003, one well-known fund management house was quoted in the *Financial Times* as saying, "Chinese demand for commodities is revolutionising global commodity markets. China has already overtaken the USA as the largest consumer of iron ore, steel and copper." The *Financial Times* concludes, "The China effect seems unstoppable." As with peak oil, the mistake that commodity forecasters make is assuming that the recent past is a good guide to what could happen in the future. As Phillip Tetlock and Michael Horowitz pointed out when reviewing the National Intelligence Council's *Global Trends* series, "The reports almost inevitably fall into the trap of treating the conventional wisdom of the present as the blueprint for the future 15 or 20 years down the road."[50]

In the decade following the creation of the BRIC moniker, the group surged as a global economic power, only to eventually suffer a sharp reversal of fortunes. In a 2011 report from Goldman Sachs, the investment bank stated that the economic potential for BRICs probably peaked because of a smaller supply of new workers. However, other factors have emerged that cast doubt on their performance in the past and their potential for the future. Brazil has suffered a corruption scandal and is showing all of the symptoms of the commodity resource curse that has afflicted other economies. International sanctions have been placed on Russia following its military transgressions. China, long an engine of the world's growth slowed to its weakest expansion since 1990. Perhaps the brightest outlook is in India, but even here reforms have been sclerotic. Even Goldman Sachs lamented the over-hyping of the BRICs phenomenon. After haemorrhaging losses for five years straight, their BRICs fund was quietly dissolved in August 2015.[51][52]

Oil super-spike

Forecasts from sources that are believed to be "credible" can gain plenty of attention from the media and investors. But, remember, the message might be twisted from the way the original research intended.[53]

One such example comes from the summer of 2008. Oil prices had just risen above $100 per barrel. Noting that prices had advanced more quickly than they had forecast back in 2005, the investment bank Goldman Sachs issued a note suggesting that the high end of its forecast range was now $135 a barrel – but they also hinted that prices could go much higher: "As the lack of supply growth and price-insulated non-OECD [Organisation for Economic Co-operation and Development] demand suggest a future rebound in U.S. gross domestic product growth or a major oil supply disruption could lead to $150-$200 a barrel oil prices." Goldman Sachs continued, "The possibility of $150-$200 per barrel seems increasingly likely over the next six-24 months, [in the case of] a major disruption." "The core of our 'super-spike' view is that oil prices will keep rising until demand declines globally on a multi-year basis, resulting in the return of excess capacity and a lower cost structure," Goldman Sachs' analysts said. "Given this view, once excess capacity returns, we think prices can move sharply lower."[54]

In their defence, Goldman Sachs never said that oil prices would reach $200 per barrel, only that prices *could* reach that price in the event of a "major disruption". However, the media interpreted the research with the headlines "Oil Could Hit $200 in 'Super-Spike'" and "An Oracle of Oil Predicts $200-a-Barrel Crude".

So why did Goldman Sachs' research note gain such credibility and such misinterpretation? In 2004, Goldman Sachs' analyst Arjun Murti concluded that the world was headed for a prolonged supply shock that would push prices through the roof. Murti predicted that, although Western countries were discussing the need to reduce energy consumption, there was still no sign of the excess production capacity needed to cool the market. That summer, as oil traded for approximately $40 a barrel, Mr Murti coined what has become his signature phrase: "super-spike". The following March, he drew further attention by predicting that prices could soar to $105 as part of his "super-spike" oil theory, sending shock waves through the market.

Angry investors questioned whether Goldman Sachs' own oil traders benefited from the prediction. At Goldman Sachs' annual meeting,

Henry M. Paulson Jr., at the time the bank's Chief Executive, defended Murti. "Our traders were as surprised as everyone else was," Paulson reportedly said. "Our research department is totally independent. Our trading departments have no say about this." Murti, for his part, agrees, discounting suggestions that his reports and others like it affect market prices. "Whenever an analyst upgrades a stock or downgrades a stock, sometimes you get a reaction that day, but beyond a day, fundamentals win out," he said. Irrespective of if and how the bank profited from the forecast moving the market the message for investors is that you need to be careful about how research is presented and has been interpreted by others.

Not in my lifetime

Fast forward to early 2016. The price of oil had fallen towards $30 per barrel after falling relentlessly from over $110 per barrel only 18 months earlier. With oil prices so low, pundit Dennis Gartman, appeared on TV stating that: "We won't see crude above $44 again in my lifetime." Gartman is an omnipresent voice on the 24 hour business news coverage. He is the publisher of the *Gartman Letter*, a daily markets newsletter, which is, according to his website, read by "leading banks, brokerage firms, hedge funds, mutual funds and energy and grain trading firms around the world."

Now, Gartman is no spring chicken and perhaps he knew something we didn't, but only three months later oil prices had rebounded to $45 per barrel. Pity those investors that placed too much emphasis on Gartman's forecasts. Still alive, but perhaps not with his credibility, Gartman appeared again with an explanation:[55]

Finally... and perhaps most

importantly... we invoke Lord John Maynard Keynes this morning who said long ago when he had changed his mind on an investment he had previous touted that "When the facts change, I change; What then do you do, Sir?" The facts are changing in the world of crude oil; demand is still rather strong and supplies seem to be rising but only modestly. Further, the term structures are shifting. We had been, on balance and really quite openly, bearish of crude for the past several years, erring always to sell crude's rallies rather than to buy crude's weakness. That has been wrong for the past two months and it is time to acknowledge that "wrongness". If the facts are indeed changing... and certainly they seem to be... then we too must change. Lord Keynes did; we must also.

Although conciliatory, acknowledging his mistakes, you would have thought that Gartman would learn from making such bombastic calls. You would think that the TV networks that propagate his views would put someone on who was more accurate in his or her predictions. And you would think that investors would be turned by his inability to provide them with any clue over where they should put their capital. But alas, no. Fast forward another few months and Gartman appears again with another prediction. This time that "investors shouldn't expect the commodity to break through $55 for a few years."[56]

Gartman's calls on markets of all sorts are the stuff of ridicule. From crude to equity markets to bonds and currencies, Gartman has made some eye catching but incorrect forecasts. The pundit has got so much attention that many investors track his calls, but most likely only for ridicule. So why does he still get so much attention? What aspect of his forecasts means he can appear on TV while others, perhaps more accurate and astute observers of commodity markets, get much less attention? It should be clear by now that "one-handed" pundits are not on TV to impart trading and investing knowledge. Networks have to occupy airtime and so they bring telegenic persons who use this chance to raise their profile and get free publicity for their services.

Monetary collapse

Every morning before he left home, the illusionist James Randi used to take a piece of paper and write on it, "I James Randi will die today". He'd then sign and date it and slip it in the pocket of his jacket. Had he died, of course, the world would be full of credulous believers insisting he was a genuine psychic seer. Every day, across the world, people predict that markets will boom, bust or stagger sideways like a drunken sailor. Eventually one of their predictions comes true and gullible people everywhere equate this with foresight when, in fact, the forecaster has simply been slipping a note in their pocket each morning. In a world where everyone predicts everything, occasionally someone's going to be right.[57]

More than any other commodity, gold seems to involve a stream of fantastic tales of imminent financial or societal collapse. Every potential problem gets blown up into a coming apocalypse. Fiat currency leads to worldwide collapse as the dollar falters and hyperinflation appears. All paper money will be worthless, so you better have some gold if you want to protect your wealth and be able to feed your family. Gold is often marketed through a combination of fear and dishonesty.

Much like a cult, higher gold prices justify the investment. Lower gold prices prompt more investment, since non-believers aren't buying. The lack of Armageddon, meanwhile, only serves to embolden believers that the time will come. Here is how Izabella Kaminska, in the excellent *Financial Times Alphaville* blog, describes gold bugs relationship with the metal:[58]

> Goldbugs don't just believe in the fundamentals of gold. They worship at the altar of gold. The goldbug view represents a market philosophy, a doctrine and a belief-system. Question it and you incite anger, rage, ridicule.
>
> For "non-believers" this can be frustrating. It's impossible to have a rational discussion on the subject because goldbugs inevitably intervene with "absolute" views, none of which are open to adjustment. They stick to those absolutes, even if the facts don't fit [sic] support the narrative.

As with the cult in Michigan, market participants and commodity market forecasters are open to failure denial too. "The New Case for Gold" by James Rickards, published right after the price of gold fell by 33% from its 2011 high, is one example. Rickards believes it is inevitable that gold prices will rise toward $10,000 per ounce, and possibly even to $50,000 per ounce. Much like Randi's signed paper in his pocket, Rickards regular web bulletins predicting the collapse of the incumbent monetary order are delivered in a tone of high intensity and deep intrigue. He often relays nuggets of encounters with mysterious insiders and high officials deep inside the world's monetary policy and finance elites, the defence and intelligence community, and international figures of hinted-at glamorous background.[59]

Gold is a "fiat commodity" – one that has value as an asset if, and to the extent that, enough people believe it has value. Like paper, currency gold is "irredeemable". It is an "outside" asset – an asset of the holder that is not a liability of anyone else. As a fiat commodity currency, gold's value will be determined by its attractiveness relative to other fiat currencies – the fiat paper currencies issued by central banks. In this way, gold should not be analysed in the same way as another commodity, but as part of a set of fiat currencies – the US dollar and the Euro, etc. Gold will be most attractive when market participants are most nervous about the future value of other fiat currencies. Concern among investors grows when governments appear to be spending too much (ie, increasing the size of their budget deficit) and/or when central banks do not do enough to contain rising prices – inflation, of course, erodes the purchasing value of currency.

As Willem Middelkoop describes in his book "*The Big Reset*", no monetary system lasts forever. The global monetary system has changed before – the end of the gold standard, for example – and the current fiat monetary system could well be replaced in the future. But what that means is that, like every other forecast, you should be aware of the risks of it not happening as predicted. As with all commodity forecasts, if the gold forecaster believes it's a one-way bet then run a mile.[60]

I'll leave this section with a quote from the hedge fund manager Paul Brodsky: "Gold is intrinsically worthless or intrinsically priceless…You can build a financial model to value it, but every input is just going to be your imagination."[61]

Interest in themes passes as prices fall

If you search on Google for news search terms referencing "peak oil" you get a line with spikes, very similar to the price of oil. Higher oil prices leading to an increase in people's perception of scarcity and so interest in the potential causes of that trend. Likewise, since the drop in the price of oil from mid-2014, searches in Google for "peak oil" have dropped as well. By early 2015, Google searches for "too much oil" had outstripped those for "peak oil". This serves to illustrate the short termism in many commodity markets. Investors change their focus from one aspect of the market to another – the change in sentiment often whipsawing commodity prices.[62]

This change in emphasis by commodity market participants also serves to illustrate why it's difficult to extrapolate the past to the future. The things that have mattered to commodity traders and investors in the past may not matter to the same degree in the immediate future, and so investors expecting changes in economic and commodity market variables to have a similar impact on the price of a commodity may be disappointed.

Earlier in this chapter, I discussed the books, publications and stories of Malthus, Ehrlich and other pundits of their day. The publication of their works has often marked the high point in the market – from wheat prices in the late eighteenth century, concerns over famine in the 1970s and low oil prices in the late 1990s. What will be next?

The relative ease by which authors can publish their works does not seem to work against this counter cyclical trend. Instead, it may have sped up. Now, more than ever, it is possible to jump on the bandwagon of commodity price trends and call yourself a prescient pundit. One conclusion is that investors should keep track of the books that are being published as they appear to represent a good signal of a change in the prevailing price trend.

Forecasters are storytellers and not diviners of the future. Like all authors of fiction, we should enjoy them for what they are. But that begs the next question. Who are they?

Chapter 6: Pundits, Forecasters and Soothsayers

"No matter how much evidence exists that seers do not exist, suckers will pay for the existence of seers."

J. Scott Armstrong

Who are the commodity forecasters? Understanding the incentives of the commodity forecaster means it's possible to understand their behaviour, the biases they may fall foul of and how you can be a better consumer of their forecasts.

The investment bank

Investment banks have traditionally provided research – whether that relates to commodities or other assets like equities, bonds and currencies, etc – to their clients for free. Research also serves as marketing material for the bank too. You will often see reports on financial TV and the press highlighting research that one or another bank has just published.

There are two main problems with the market being dominated by big investment banks providing free research to their clients. First, there's a potential conflict of interest, ie, the providers may benefit from those same clients acting upon their predictions. For example, a bullish commodity market outlook will benefit other parts of the bank with an interest in investors "buying in" to a positive growth story. This could involve a miner looking to an investment bank to secure more funding from capital markets. This could mean, in theory, that commodity analysts adjust their price forecasts up, making it more likely that the deal to secure funding for the miner succeeds and is more profitable for the bank in terms of fees. Second, since the research was free there is no market to speak of, no real incentive to get the forecasts right. Without a competitive market for the price predictions and the underlying analysis to be as accurate as possible, then there is little incentive to improve.

The financial media will often pick up on a story that one or another famous investor or investment bank is bullish on this or bearish on that. Should you follow them blindly and invest? No, absolutely not. You don't know what level of risk they are taking to enter that position. Have they hedged it and how? Do they even have any "skin-in-the-game" anyway and are following up their forecast with a position in the market? The best investors should also be able to change their minds if the evidence no longer supports their original hypothesis, and the same can be said for institutions that publish price forecasts. However, if the bank changes its mind will it get picked up by the press, or even get published? It might do, but it might not.

Cullen Roche of Orcam Financial Group and the excellent *Pragmatic Capitalism* blog makes the point that without understanding the incentives belying their forecast, individual investors might get into big trouble:

> In all seriousness, the key lesson here is that we need to be very careful about how much we read into news headlines about market gurus. It's very easy to get swept up in the idea that a wealthy investor knows more than the rest of us and that we should follow their *disclosed* moves as reported

and after the fact. The financial media loves to use big names to grab headlines and page views. But in many cases you're not getting the full story about what this investor is doing. And following their supposed positioning could lead to bad decisions and unnecessarily poor performance.[63]

Think about why the financial media publish forecasts next time you see them on TV or on the internet. Are they to help inform those not fortunate enough to be able to afford buying their forecasts off the shelf? Are they meant as "entertainment", as a way of gathering publicity to sell other "services"? Or are they setting up the sucker to invest in a particular commodity market, just as the forecaster has pulled out of the market or, even worse, is on the other side of the trade?

The independent

Various consultancies operate in different commodity markets. Often they might be involved in collecting prices for opaque commodity markets, while using their experience and understanding of the underlying physical market to provide forecasts. Others might operate outside of commodity markets altogether, relying on their macroeconomic skills and models to provide forecasts.

To varying degrees these commodity forecasters can be seen as the most independent from the actual market, since they have much less incentive to tailor the forecast to suit their client base or a position that they hold. On the flip side, perhaps, these forecasters have nothing in the way of "skin-in-the-game" as an incentive to get the forecast correct.

The physical commodity producer/trader

Miners, commodity trading houses and others often release their own forecasts of where they expect one or a range of commodity prices to be in the near or long-term future. In the case of a mining company, these forecasts might be released around the same time as annual reports detailing the company's activities are published, or when they are trying to raise funding for new investments. These forecasts can be said to have "skin-in-the-game", with many commodity investors hanging on every word for clues as to how underlying physical demand and supply is likely to evolve. On the flip side, it's difficult to argue that they are an unbiased prediction of commodity prices.

It's not unreasonable to assume that a buyer (perhaps a large airline wanting to buy aluminium) or a seller (a miner/smelter of industrial metals) of commodities must have a much stronger incentive to have an accurate view of where a commodity market is heading, and inside information about their actual demand and supply in order to produce better predictions. However, that's not what the evidence finds. Wishful thinking is a powerful factor in adversely affecting forecasting ability.

The economist Guy Mayraz conducted a simple experiment, at Oxford University's Centre for Experimental Social Science, to test how "skin-in-the-game" affected the accuracy of predictions. Mayraz ran sessions in which the participants were shown ninety days of historical wheat price data and were then asked to predict the price of wheat on the one-hundredth day. Besides being paid a bonus for accurate forecasts, half the experimental subjects were told that they were "bakers" who would profit if the price of wheat fell, and the other half were told they were "farmers" who would make money if the price of wheat rose.[64]

Logically, in the study a "farmer" should make the same forecast as a "baker", since the forecast does not change the outcome and both of them are paid for accuracy. However, that's not what Mayraz found. Instead, nearly two-thirds of "farmers" predicted higher-than-average prices and nearly two-thirds of "bakers" predicted lower-than-average prices. Even when the scale of the bonus was increased, Mayraz found no significant increase in forecast accuracy. It seems that wishful thinking can get you into a lot of trouble.

To herd or not to herd

Forecasters are exposed to other incentives that may influence their behaviour. Any change is difficult to embrace and variables like commodity demand and supply are very difficult to understand, let alone predict. As much as you or I like to think of ourselves as forward-looking, we are all backward-looking and we update our perception of the world only gradually (known as adaptive expectations).

Take the example of oil. In the first few years of the twenty-first century, painful memories of the long period of low prices in the 1990s held back plans to expand production, even as prices surged. More recently, the production and investment plans of the major oil companies appear to have been based on the assumption that the period of high prices experienced between 2011 and mid-2014 would be sustained indefinitely. When prices have been high and rising for some time, it becomes an entrenched assumption that these high prices will persist for the foreseeable future. The point is that people typically expect the future to be like the past and they underestimate the potential for change.

Known as the recency bias, forecasters often give greater weight to very recent events in their forecast and let what could just be random events colour their perception of how the future will evolve. As the evidence of ten years of oil price predictions show, the same biases affect commodity forecasters. In benign market conditions there is an institutional inertia - only updating their view of the world slowly and iteratively, not wanting to appear too far from the pack or consensus. The exception to this appears to be when markets reach a peak or a trough. Then investment banks and commentators, etc, all want to come up with an even more extreme prediction of where prices could go.

As we saw with the oil price predictions, however, sometimes, someone consistently likes to stick their neck out with an extreme call – sticking with it through thick and thin, even when the market has clearly moved on. Researchers at the European University Viadrina Frankfurt (EUVF) analysed over 20,000 forecasts of nine different metal prices over different forecasting horizons during the fifteen years between 1995 and 2011. Instead of finding the institutional inertia and forecasting herding that we might expect, they found strong evidence of "anti-herding".[65]

So why might some forecasters want to stray from the herd? According to the EUVF paper it all comes down to incentives; and the incentive to herd or stay away depend upon the mix of clients, both existing and prospective. Think about who buys commodity forecasts. There are two groups of buyers. The first are those that buy forecasts regularly, perhaps as part of a subscription to a company's analysis or for free as clients of an investment bank, for example. Examples of frequent buyers of commodity forecasts might include an oil company or a manufacturing company that regularly buys a certain small range of commodities. Given they are long-time consumers, they may have based their decision on how accurate a forecaster was over several forecasting periods.

In contrast to the regular buyer, there are also onetime or irregular consumers of commodity price predictions. This second group of buyer is more likely to be swayed by the commodity forecaster that was most accurate in the past year or so, or has been the most vocal about his or her success. This is rational from the irregular buyer's point of view in that perhaps movements in the price of copper or another commodity only have a minor impact on their business, or maybe they only need to buy or take a view on a commodity infrequently. Either way, the cost/benefit of monitoring whether the commodity forecast they are buying has been accurate in the longer term is much higher than in the first group of buyers.

If the second group of buyers dominates (the infrequent consumer), forecasters have a strong incentive to differentiate their forecasts from the predictions of others by making extreme (or non-consensus) predictions. Even though an extreme forecast may have a small probability of being accurate, the expected payoff of such a forecast can be high, since the number of other pundits making the same extreme prediction is likely to be small. Should they be successful in their prediction, then the forecaster can capture the attention and the wallets of the infrequent consumer of forecasts.

In contrast, if a forecaster publishes a less

extreme forecast, one close to the consensus forecast, then by definition there is a high probability that other forecasters will make similar forecasts. If this is the case then even if a forecaster's price prediction is spot on, then the impact on his income and reputation will be minimal. The infrequent buyer will ask, "why pay for a forecast from an average forecaster?"

Incentives, being as they are, set up a paradox. For just as commodity prices work on reflexivity, the same could be true of the commodity forecaster. While a single or a string of successful predictions will bolster a forecaster's reputation, this may result in future forecasts being much less extreme in order to protect their reputation. When a person or a company has their name on a forecast that may also alter the incentives; for example, a commodity research firm with a relatively low profile (perhaps it is just moving into the area) would be rational to make a wild forecast, drawing big attention from the media. In contrast, firms with a strong reputation are likely to make much more conservative forecasts, not wanting to stray too far away from the consensus.

Herding behaviour isn't specific to explaining how the commodity forecasting firm appears to the outside world, it can also affect internal incentives. Career concerns can also play a part too. Just as at the level of the firm (whether a bank, consultancy or something else), you might think there is the temptation for an analyst to produce a bold prediction. If the analyst makes an "outlier" forecast that turns out to be spot on, this is likely to capture a lot of attention in the financial media, raising the prospect of the analyst being recruited by a rival firm touting a bigger salary and an even bigger bonus.

However, set against this is the risk of being fired (or at least having a few rungs taken from under the career progression of a young analyst) for a bad call.

To examine what the age and experience of the forecaster has on the degree of herding, research published in the RAND Journal of Economics examined over 8,000 forecasts by equity analysts between 1983 and 1996. Equity analysts *should* produce reliable forecasts of future earnings of the companies that they monitor, which are then used to produce recommendations on what their clients should buy. Equity analysts face their own quandary, having to balance the interests of the buy-side (ie, their clients who prefer accurate forecasts) and those on the sell-side (other parts of the same bank they work for that might value trading commissions and large initial public offerings more than the accuracy of their analysts forecasts). Note that commodity analysts may face their own conflicting internal objectives too. From trading commissions on a commodity-related exchange traded fund, to a bank's own proprietary trading on commodities and on to gaining profitable consulting business from a highly valued client. There is more than one incentive.[66]

What the researchers found is that younger analysts tend to herd more than their more experienced colleagues do. Less experienced analysts, meanwhile, are more heavily punished for getting their forecasts wrong and so they have every incentive to stick with the herd. In contrast, older analysts, who have presumably built up their reputations, face less risk of termination. The researchers also found that, contrary to expectations, making bold and accurate predictions does not significantly improve a young analyst's career prospects.

The final type of herding is known as investigative herding. Investigative herding arises when investors trade similarly by reacting to the arrival of a commonly observed information signal. Analysts have an incentive to investigate a piece of information or a market that he knows other analysts may also investigate and trade in. From the point of view of getting a return on the forecast, there is no incentive to build a position in a particular market if other investors won't join on the same side and push the price in the direction of the forecast. Illiquid markets tend to be less well served precisely because it is not worthwhile for banks and other financial institutions to trade them. It follows that the reputational risk of making forecasts about illiquid and volatile commodity markets is much higher.

A market for lemons?

There is another factor to consider when thinking about forecasts. Again it comes down to the incentives of the forecaster, but this time the inference is more insidious. The nature of forecasting may drive out those that are best equipped to produce them. Commodity price forecasts might just be a market for lemons. This reference to lemons comes from economist George Akerlof, who published a paper in 1970 in the *Quarterly Journal of Economics* called "The Market for Lemons". Within it was a simple and revolutionary idea in which he noted that markets in which buyers possess imperfect information while sellers possess a profit motive are thin, insubstantial and low quality.[67]

Akerlof used the example of the used-car market. Suppose buyers in the used-car market value good cars – referred to as "peaches" – at $20,000, while sellers value them slightly less. A malfunctioning used car – a "lemon" –

is worth only $10,000 to buyers (and, again, assume a bit less to sellers). If buyers can tell "lemons" and "peaches" apart, trade in both will flourish. In reality, buyers might struggle to tell the difference: scratches can be touched up, engine problems left undisclosed, even odometers tampered with.

To account for the risk that a car is a lemon, therefore, buyers cut their offers. They might be willing to pay, say, $15,000 for a car they perceive as having an even chance of being a "lemon" or a "peach". But dealers who know for sure they have a "peach" will reject such an offer. As a result, the buyers face "adverse selection": the only sellers who will be prepared to accept $15,000 will be those who know they are offloading a "lemon".

Smart buyers can foresee this problem. With the knowledge that they will only ever be sold a "lemon", they offer only $10,000. Sellers of "lemons" end up with the same price as they would have done were there no ambiguity. However, the "peaches" stay in the garage. This is a tragedy: there are buyers who would happily pay the asking price for a "peach", if only they could be sure of the car's quality. This "information asymmetry" between buyers and sellers kills the market.

In the same way as the used-car market example, one could argue that bad forecasters drive out good forecasters. The deep uncertainty that forecasting fosters may create incentives that perversely degrade the ability to offer better predictions. Many bright individuals might be deterred from working in the sector because, as we've seen, from a career perspective the likelihood of error is so high. You could argue that there is little incentive to contribute when the exercise is seen as a dubious one. This then creates the space for people who are less afraid of such reputational costs, which in the end only results in a less critical debate.

There is also little incentive for forecasters to improve on their predictions. Rather, the incentives are geared towards exaggerating the precision of forecasts – a form of signalling in economics parlance. Just as with second-hand car dealers, the job market and many other markets, there is an asymmetry of information. In order to correct for this, dealers, job seekers and perhaps forecasters may try to signal their trustworthiness and talents by collecting awards that convey some authority – the best second-hand car dealer in the North West, for example, or the best gold price forecaster of the last quarter. Such exaggerations satiate the cognitive preferences of governments and corporations, and generate greater media attention to the forecast itself.

For much of the private sector, public forecasts are designed to maximise marketing rather than predictive accuracy. As Philip Tetlock concluded:

> ...the demand for accurate predictions is insatiable. Reliable suppliers are few and far between. And this gap between demand and supply creates opportunities for unscrupulous suppliers to fill the void by gulling desperate customers into thinking they are getting something no one else knows how to provide.

So are commodity forecasts worth paying for? The evidence suggests that the answer is no. The underlying incentives also suggest the answer is no. So what gives? Why does the market still exist? In a paper published in

Technology Review in 1980, J. Scott Armstrong examined the reason why people are willing to pay heavily for advice about the future from "expert" forecasters. The paper, entitled "The Seer-Sucker Theory: The Value of Experts in Forecasting", found that by looking through the available evidence and beyond a minimal level of expertise there is little improvement in forecasting ability. In fact, forecasting accuracy seems to drop once people get above a certain level of expertise.[68]

Why, therefore, do people continue to follow, and in many cases pay for, forecasts when their record is so abysmal? Armstrong believes that one reason for this might be to do with an avoidance of responsibility on behalf of the consumer of the forecast. Investors and company executives may actively seek out predictions because they can offer a precise way of justifying investments under periods of uncertainty. This decision paralysis, as it's known, was best described by the psychologists Amon Tversky and Eldar Shafir. They uncovered situations where the mere existence of uncertainty altered how people behaved, even when the decision was irrelevant to the outcome. At the extreme, accuracy may not even count for much in the demand for price predictions. The client may not be interested in precision, but avoiding responsibility – if things don't turn out as expected, then they can always blame the "expert"! Forecasts offer a means of distancing oneself from the decision. "Look, it didn't turn out well, but all the predictions at the time said it would."

For every seer, there's a sucker.

Chapter 7: The Illusion of Knowledge

"Everything we hear is an opinion, not a fact. Everything we see is a perspective, not the truth."

Marcus Aurelius

Unlike other animals we have evolved and adapted by being able to see patterns in the weather, the stars, our behaviour and many other things and then taking advantage of those patterns in order to survive. However, recognising objects and patterns in difficult and stressful situations means generalising. Evolutionary instincts often lead us to see patterns when there are none.

The human brain is quite remarkable. It can store perhaps three terabytes of information, and yet that is only approximately one-millionth of the information that IBM says is now produced in the world each day. Therefore, we have to be terribly selective about the information we choose to remember. Alvin Toffler – author of "Future Shock", published in 1970 – predicted some of the consequences of what he called "information overload". He thought our defence mechanism would be to simplify the world in ways that confirmed our biases, even as the world itself was growing more diverse and more complex. As Nate Silver describes in his book "The Signal and the Noise":[69]

> ...if the quantity of information is increasing by 2.5 quintillion bytes per day, the amount of useful information almost certainly isn't. Most of it is just noise, and the noise is increasing faster than the

signal. There are so many hypotheses to test, so many data sets to mine — but a relatively constant amount of objective truth.

In any field of economics there is a significant amount of noise that can drown out the signal. Noise then is what can make predictions of the outlook for the economy, commodity demand and supply next quarter and the future of commodity prices much more uncertain. There is no factor, or even group of factors, that causes a commodity price to move in a certain way. According to US financial economist Fisher Black's model of the way we see the world, noise is what makes our observations imperfect:[70]

> The effects of noise on the world, and on our views of the world, are profound. Noise in the sense of a large number of small events is often a causal factor much more powerful than a small number of large events can be. Noise makes trading in financial markets possible, and thus allows us to observe prices for financial assets. Noise causes markets to be somewhat inefficient, but often prevents us from taking advantage of inefficiencies. Noise in the form of uncertainty about future tastes and technology by sector causes business cycles... Most generally, noise makes it very difficult to test either practical or academic theories about the way that financial or economic markets work. We are forced to act largely in the dark.

One of the risks that we face in the

information age is that even if the amount of information is increasing, the gap between what we know and what we think we know is widening still further. As Dan Gardner suggests in his book "Future Babble", "In fact, more information makes more explanations possible, so having lots of data available can actually empower our tendency to see things that aren't there."[71]

There is an illusion of knowledge.

Many studies have looked at this through various experiments. In one study eight experienced bookmakers were shown a list of 88 variables found on a typical past performance chart on a horse – the weight to be carried, the number of races won, the performance in different conditions, etc. They were asked to rank the pieces of information by importance. The bookmakers were then given data for the past forty races and were asked to rank the top five horses in each race. The past data was given in increments of the 5, 10, 20 and 40 variables that each bookmaker had selected as most important. Hence, each bookmaker predicted the outcome of each race four times – once for each of the information sets. For each prediction, the bookmakers were asked to give a degree of confidence ranking in their forecast.[72]

Accuracy was pretty much a flat line regardless of the amount of information the bookmakers had at their disposal. However, what happened to the bookmakers' confidence? It soared as the information set increased. With five pieces of information, accuracy and confidence were quite closely related. However, by the time 40 pieces of information were being used, accuracy was still exactly the same, but confidence soared from below 20% to almost 35%!

If examples of over-confidence exist in

estimating the probability of horses in a race then surely it exists in commodity markets, as well as other assets like equities and bonds? Part of the difficulty is being able to do a post-event review of events to see if the forecast was correct. Many commodity market investments (such as mines and deep-sea oil wells) involve billions of dollars and 20-30 year time horizons, if not more. As the amount of information about commodity markets increases, it becomes more difficult to separate the signal from the noise. However, it also becomes easier to make mistakes and, in turn, our ability to propagate those mistakes increases too.

Bounded rationality

Prices, stock levels, geopolitics, hedge fund positioning, technical indicators, strike action, weather disruptions, investment plans, interest rates, costs, resource nationalism, cartels, climate change and expectations – we are bombarded by so much information about commodities. Much of the information is contradictory, lots of it incomplete, much of it with questionable integrity – you could forgive the average person interested in the outlook for a particular commodity of suffering from cognitive overload. This is precisely what many economists believe happens to people that have to make a decision based on so much information.

The economist and political scientist Herbert Simon is most famous for his theory of bounded rationality, a principle of economic decision-making that Simon himself preferred to call "satisficing" – a combination of two words: "satisfy" and "suffice". Simon maintained that individuals do not seek to maximise their benefit from a particular course of action because they cannot assimilate and digest all of the information that would be needed. Not only can they not get access to all the information required, but even if they could their minds would be unable to process it properly. The human mind necessarily restricts itself. It is, as Simon put it, bounded by "cognitive limits". Here's Simon again:[73]

> In an information-rich world, the wealth of information means a dearth of something else: a scarcity of whatever it is that information consumes. What information consumes is rather obvious: it consumes the attention of its recipients. Hence a wealth of information creates a poverty of attention and a need to allocate that attention efficiently among the overabundance of information sources that might consume it.

The problem for the investor or decision maker in commodity markets is that they only have limited attention to make an informed decision on where the price could be going. This opens up the market for commodity forecasts, but also then means that the consumer of that forecast has limited attention to critique it properly.

Anchoring or recency bias

"In a few months, I expect to see the stock market much higher than today." These were the words of Irving Fisher – America's distinguished and famous economist and professor of economics at Yale University – only 14 days before Wall Street crashed on Black Tuesday, 29th October 1929. Only days after the crash, the Harvard Economic Society offered this analysis to its subscribers: "A severe depression such as 1920-21 is outside the range of probability. We are not facing a protracted liquidation."

Most forecasters predict a future quite like the recent past. One reason is that things generally continue as they have been, and so major changes just don't occur very often. Another reason is that most people don't do "zero-based" forecasting, but start with the current observation or normal range and then add or subtract a bit as they think is appropriate. A final reason is that real "sea changes" are extremely difficult to foretell. That's why some of the best-remembered (or infamous) forecasts are the ones that extrapolated current conditions or trends, but turned out to be badly wrong. Seismic changes in financial markets are generally unforeseen by most people.

As Lant Pritchett and Lawrence Summers note, "Many of the great economic forecasting errors of the past half century came from excessive extrapolation of performance of the recent past and treating a country's growth rate as a permanent characteristic rather than a transient condition." Clearly, a common source of error from economic forecasters has been the excessive weighting of current rates of economic growth over the tendency of countries to revert to their mean growth rate. Forecasters simply stick too closely to the current level, and on those rare occasions when they call for change, they often underestimate the potential magnitude. Very few people predicted that oil would decline significantly back in June 2014, and fewer still mentioned the possibility that we would see $60 per barrel within six months.[74]

Predictions of a persistent, durable Cold War sounded reasonable in 1984; the same prediction would have sounded less reasonable just a few years later. In the early 20th century, forecasters were warning about "peak oil" and US energy dependence on the rest of the world. Now the US is the leading producer of oil in the world and has dramatically reduced its need for oil imports. More generally, economic forecasts can over-hype short-term bursts of economic growth, overlooking the fact that such bursts tend to be transient. In short, most forecasting is done incrementally and few predictors contemplate order-of-magnitude changes.

The same bias that makes commodity forecasters use the current environment (demand, supply and price) as the baseline for a forecast also influences the behaviour of the consumer of that same forecast. This is where commodity forecasts can be especially powerful and dangerous. Research has found that even if a number is generated randomly it can still have a powerful influence on people's behaviour. For instance, Englich, Mussweiler and Strack show that when setting jail sentences, legal experts were influenced by irrelevant anchors even when they were fully aware of the irrelevance of the input. In one study, participants (judges) were asked to role dice to determine the sentencing request from the prosecution. The pair of dice they used were loaded to give either a low number (one and two) or a high number (three and six). After rolling the dice, participants were told to sum the scores and that this number represented the prosecutions demand. Since the judges themselves rolled the dice, they could clearly see that the input was irrelevant. However, those who received a total score of three issued an average sentence of 5.3 months, and those who received a total score of nine issued an average sentence of 7.8 months![75]

So, by even providing a forecast (from a random number generator perhaps or something more reasoned), people are likely to cling to it. With great power, comes great responsibility.

Availability bias

In a similar vein to the recency bias, the availability bias results in analysts and forecasters latching onto to the most prominent piece of data or information. One aspect of this bias relates to the quality of the data that exists on commodity markets. As I outlined earlier, the quality and accessibility of commodity data varies widely between different markets and countries. Take the oil market as an example. The best and most readily accessible data is for the US, and so participants in commodity markets often place excessive emphasis on it. Inevitably, analysts, traders, investors and journalists then extrapolate data from the US as representative of what is happening elsewhere in the market. As long as the US data is more accurate, detailed and timely than that for other countries, this example of "availability bias" is likely to continue.

The availability bias is perhaps even more important now than ever. In an age of streaming tweets, 24/7 financial media coverage and ease of access to investment, coupled with trading platforms on your smart-phone pinging the latest financial data, it is hard not to be swayed by the latest "significant" news story or large move in commodity markets. The danger if you fall foul of this bias is that you fail to appreciate the wider picture – a picture that might show a very different or even contradictory view of the market.

Confirmation bias

"A business opportunity is promising", "New love beckons", "A figure from the past makes contact". It's what makes horoscopes so appealing. Those that seem to fit our circumstances grab our attention and are remembered, while those that don't are scarcely noticed and quickly forgotten. Like superstition, we tend to see what we want to see, an observation that Sir Francis Bacon made well: "The root of all superstition is that men observe when a thing hits, but not when it misses."

In behavioural economics jargon, this phenomenon is known as "confirmation bias". Forecasts are often used to confirm what one already thought, how we seek out information that confirms our own worldview and reject or ignore any disconfirming evidence. Researchers at the Toulouse School of Economics and Bocconi University found that, perhaps not surprisingly, individual investors who are initially optimistic over the future price direction of an asset tend to ignore subsequent signals that conflict with their initial beliefs, and vice versa.[76]

This need to seek out confirming viewpoints is likely to stretch to subscribing or purchasing predictions from forecasters that align with your view of the world. Or, indeed, it could result in a speculator betting more and more money that a certain commodity price will increase further after subsequent forecasts continue to confirm that his first bet, that of higher prices, was a good one. Both of these actions, enabled by the confirmation bias often lead commodity investors to take short cuts. Short cuts that may lead them to paying over the odds.

Theory-induced blindness

Matthew Syed's book "Black Box Thinking" describes the case of a group of economists in

2009 warning about the risk of inflation following the US Federal Reserve's decision to pump an additional $600 billion into the US economy. The signatories to the letter were worried that the policy could be disastrous; their greatest concern being that printing money would lead to run-away price increases.[77]

At the time the letter was published, the inflation rate was 1.5%. Four years later, in December 2014, inflation had fallen to 0.8%; in early 2015, it had declined further to minus 0.1%. How did the signatories react to this decline? When the signatories to the forecast were invited to reflect on the content of their letter in light of the subsequent events, what was striking was that they did not attempt to explain why their predictions had failed. No, instead they didn't think their prediction had failed at all. "The letter was correct as stated," said one signatory. Another responded with, "I think there's plenty of inflation – not at the check-out, necessarily, but on Wall Street." Meanwhile, when asked about inflation, a third responded by saying, "They are going to go above 2%. I don't know when, but they will."

Cognitive dissonance is a psychological phenomenon that refers to the discomfort felt at a discrepancy between what you already believe to be true and new information that presents itself. This is an especially big risk for forecasters of all types, but essentially means that the forecaster will either discount new information that conflicts with the stated forecast or attempt to reframe the evidence to validate the success of the forecast.

There is nothing wrong with making mistakes in commodity forecasting. As we've seen during this book, the world is complex and there are many uncertainties. But instead of questioning their initial logic or trying to understand why events may not have panned out how they expected, the signatories failed to admit that they were wrong.

In chapter 3, I introduced the main ways that commodity forecasters look to predict the outlook for commodity prices. Scepticism about the use of methods to predict the future path of commodity prices does not come easily, especially if you were responsible for building the model. This barrier to recognising the flaws in your model of the way the world works is known as "theory-induced blindness".

Anas Alhajji is an energy economist and the Managing Partner at Energy Outlook Advisers. When I interviewed Alhajji for this book, one of the main concerns he shared with me was how theory-induced blindness is still pervasive in much of the research on forecasting commodity prices:

> Most of the best research on forecasting etc. comes from universities. If you are a young professor, you need to publish. If your work is not main stream, you cannot be published. Therefore, you cannot get promotion and you cannot be tenured. The elders in the field are the referees of these articles and control the journals. So the literature is naturally biased toward older research. Also, as a young researcher, you need to get funding. Only certain ideas are funded. That is another bias.

How does this bias affect forecasting models? Well, according to Alhajji, the researchers and particularly those that sign off on the research have their eyes firmly in the rear view mirror:

"Too much politics have been inserted into the modeling of commodities, especially oil. Take the example of OPEC literature. Models developed in the early 1970s based on the Arab embargo are still in use today."

In an article for *Project Syndicate*, Alhajji highlights the inconvenient truth about many oil price forecasts:[78]

> Current forecasting models project world oil demand based on variables such as economic growth (or income), oil prices, the price of oil substitutes, and past demand. They also project non-OPEC output using variables such as oil prices, production costs, and past supply. But, after forecasting world demand and non-OPEC supply, these models simply assume that OPEC will supply the rest - without taking into account OPEC behavior or considering that OPEC members might not be willing or able to meet the "residual" demand. For this reason, these models estimate what is known as the "call on OPEC," the difference between estimated world demand and estimated non-OPEC supply.

Prior to the energy crisis of the 1970s, few economists were paying much attention to the oil sector. The magnitude of the crisis attracted economists from a wide array of specialities, as Alhajji describes:

> To diagnose the problem, they opened their toolkit and use what was available: if the supply and demand model did not work, then the monopoly model would. Economists,

politicians, and the media thus found the term "cartel" to be highly convenient. According to the monopoly model, the cartel would always supply the difference between total demand and the output supplied by non-cartel members. Although the situation has changed drastically since the early 1970's, and the cartel model has been proved wrong and harmful, it is still used today.

Loss aversion

The financial media, like individual investors and pundits, reflect a collective mood regarding the state of the market. This is important to understand because it can provide the context behind the way that forecasts are presented in the media. In theory, the relationship between word choice and the markets should be linear. Taking equity markets as an example, the higher markets go, the more positive the language should become. Conversely, when markets fall, the language should grow more negative. This was the message from earlier research from the economist Robert Shiller, who explained in his book "Irrational Exuberance" that the media tend to exaggerate average days, hyping up stocks on very strong days, as much as they overdid the gloom in bad times.[79]

A paper published in 2017 by Diego Garcia of the University of Colorado, entitled "The Kinks of Financial Journalism", shows that, at least based on word choice, this relationship does hold, but only up to a point. As the title of his paper suggests, what Professor Garcia found was that market reporters tended to be asymmetric in the way they report market moves. The media are more negative about market falls than they are positive about market rises. But as markets rise above a certain point or for a certain length of time, they reach a "kink" in which higher market highs made little or no difference to the positivity of journalists' prose. However, as price falls grew worse, the language grew ever more negative.[80]

The methodology involved searching through a database of financial market stories published by the *New York Times* and the *Wall Street Journal* between 1905 and 2005. The researchers assigned a score to the choice of words on a scale from positive to negative and then analysed how the positivity and negativity of coverage correlated with moves in the Dow Jones Industrial Average (DJIA). While the DJIA does not represent an average investor's portfolio by any means, and is a measure of equity markets rather than commodities, it is reasonable to assume that the language of financial media reporting is similar across different asset classes. The caveat being that the price of commodities depends on the context, for while investors in energy producers may like higher oil prices, major energy importing nations will not since it could be a drag on economic growth.

As markets rise, investor confidence increases. Unknowingly, this higher confidence triggers perceptions of greater certainty and control among the media and investors alike. Cognitively, the brain is at greater and greater ease and rational thought takes a back seat. As a result, with things going well, we require little third party explanation or validation. Good times don't need a story, let alone encouraging and positive language. There is little the financial media can or need add to the cognitive sensation that good has become better and the only way is up. For investors, the fact that the market was up and then up some more is itself self-affirming. Inherently investors want rising markets to be normal. In fact, ideally, rising markets should be so normal as to be altogether "un-newsworthy". So, after a few days, there is remarkably little for the media to offer.

Falling markets, however, are a very different story. As markets fall, investor confidence decreases. Cognitive strain quickly develops and, as a result, narratives become vital as investors seek out reasons to be confident. Ironically, the media rarely offers that. As the media reflects the same falling mood and growing uncertainty as its followers, its own articles and stories become more negative as market prices decline. As peculiar as this may sound, by growing more and more negative the media is affirming that investors are correct in their feelings of uncertainty and being out of control. The lesson for investors and physical buyers and sellers in commodity markets is to recognise the change in the language used as a means for spotting euphoria and despair.

According to the *Financial Times* journalist John Authors, the financial media is exposed to asymmetrical incentives. The media are affected by "what might be a variation on what is known in the behavioural finance world as 'loss aversion'." The financial media, reflecting the fears of investors, are horrified at the prospect of losses and reflect this in their reporting. Authors also believes that there is a bias in favour of caution and negativity:

> For market journalists it means that we are far more scared of encouraging readers to buy and ushering them into a loss, than we are of urging them to be cautious, and thereby leading them to miss out on a gain. I hate the fact that I

have been incorrectly bearish many times over the past eight years. But I am still deeply relieved that I was correctly bearish ahead of the disasters of 2008.

Not warning about an impending financial disaster, or at least advising caution, keeps financial journalists awake at night. The same can be said for other professions where extreme events happen – weather forecasters, for example. It is bad not to let people know about a nice sunny day in prospect, but it is unthinkable not to alert them to a serious storm in prospect. They must always err on the side of caution. For those who might doubt this, there is the sad case of Michael Fish.

Mr Fish, one of the BBC's principal weather forecasters for many years, has the immense bad luck to be remembered for one disastrous mistake. On October 15th 1987, he opened the broadcast by reassuring a viewer who had heard that there was a hurricane on the way. "Don't worry, there isn't," he said. A few hours later, the south coast of Britain was hit by a devastating storm — an event that would normally be expected to happen only once every two centuries. It caused huge damage across a swath of southern England and has forever marred Mr Fish's reputation. Fish did warn that the south coast was in for some very windy weather, but the damage was done by that over-confident opening sound bite.

Bad forecasts have consequences – either leading to complacency or over compensating for a scenario that never materialises. Falling for a convincing, but ultimately biased narrative can lead to billions of dollars of investment going down the drain. It can lock both producers and consumers into a bad deal that lasts for decades, but is ultimately a bad investment. It's to these real world consequences that we turn to in Chapter 8.

Chapter 8: White Elephants

"It's frightening to think that you might not know something, but more frightening to think that, by and large, the world is run by people who have faith that they know exactly what's going on."

Amos Tversky

The commodity industry is disparaged by many as being the laughing stock of capital allocation. As commodity prices rise higher and higher, more and more capital is allocated by investors emboldened by higher commodity prices and the notion that things are different this time. Inevitably, sooner or later, they are not.

Expectations of ever-rising commodity prices in the early twenty-first century were not without cost or impact. The commodities boom, supported by investors (most likely including a large proportion of your pension fund), allocated capital to miners, energy producers and agricultural producers who then increased the supply of every resource under the sun. Spending on resources grew so rapidly that during the 2003-15 super-cycle it exceeded 6% of global GDP for only the second time in a century.[81]

Now, in retrospect, many of these investments can be viewed as a huge mis-allocation of capital. From its peak in April 2011, the MSCI ACWI Commodity Producers Index fell 54% through its trough in January of 2016.[82] The resource sector lost $2 trillion in cumulative shareholder value in 2015 alone. Individual companies saw billions of dollars wiped off their market value, as what was once seen as fair value based on the outlook for the price of a particular commodity was subsequently seen as woefully optimistic.

The commodity bust had its upside, of course. The increase in supply that followed (higher crude oil output in the US, record breaking grain stocks, the ramp up in new sources of metal supplies) led to lower prices for you and I (or at least price increases that were not as high as they would have been). Without the crash in commodity prices, scarce financial capital could not have been allocated to more productive uses; meaning that infrastructure could now be developed at a fraction of the cost of just a few years earlier, while the *average* standard of living for individuals was higher than if commodity prices had stayed elevated.

It would be foolish to believe, however, that this was all good news. Many producers – both companies and countries – are struggling to deal with the aftermath. For example, the loss of livelihoods for those who depend on the income from the production of commodities, the loss of finance to companies that did have a viable business plan but couldn't get the funding, and the environmental damage from resource extraction that didn't need to take place. Indeed, the economic wellbeing of whole countries came down just like a pile of sand.

Investment manias are an essential part of the capitalist system. Without them we miss out on the potential upsides that can also have long lasting benefits for society and our economies. In the nineteenth century, for example, the canal and railroad booms in North America and Europe led to far lower transportation costs, from which our economies have greatly benefited ever since. The investor Marc Faber agrees:[83]

> My view is that capital spending booms like these, which inevitably lead to minor or major investment manias, are a necessary and integral

part of the capitalistic system. They drive progress and development, lower production costs, and increase productivity, even if there is inevitably some pain in the bust that follows every boom.

The risk for investors, industries, economies and individual communities and families is, however, that the boom turns from a "real world" bubble that is relatively contained within a certain industry or region into a financial bubble. And here the impact can be much greater. According to Faber:

> ...whereas every bubble will create some "white elephant" investments – investments that don't make any economic sense under any circumstances – in financial economies' bubbles, the quantity and aggregate size of "white elephant" investments is of such a colossal magnitude that the economic benefits arising from every investment boom can be more than offset by the money and wealth destruction that arise during the bust.

The term "white elephants" is defined as "a burdensome possession; creating more trouble than it's worth." In the commodity world, they could equally be defined as holes in the ground, packed full of investors' money, never to be seen again; grand projects built on a tower of sand that may have looked like the perfect thing to do at the time, but alas are now a burden.

The next part of this chapter looks at a number of those "white elephants", including examples from the dairy industry, minor metals and petrochemicals. It looks at what we knew, who said what, what happened and what the implications are.

Dairy

In the preface for this book I introduced a brief snapshot of the devastation that the over expansion of the dairy industry in New Zealand had on livelihoods, individual communities and the New Zealand economy overall. Expectations of insatiable demand don't just influence the market for copper, zinc and coal, they also affect things that you wouldn't necessarily consider to be a commodity. For the farmers of New Zealand, higher demand from China was also a big opportunity. The South Pacific nation is the world's biggest exporter of milk-based products. This looked like an ideal set of circumstances to capitalise on the promise of a seemingly never-ending demand for dairy products as Chinese consumers gradually turned to more "Western" style diets that are higher in protein.

Taking a product, assuming rising demand for it and multiplying by 1.3 billion Chinese consumers can be a risky game. To meet China's seemingly insatiable demand for ice cream, infant formula and other dairy products, New Zealand's farmers ramped up production. In the years leading up to 2013 farmers went on a buying spree, increasing their herds and buying land, and converted sheep and beef farms to dairy.

In late 2013, many industry commentators were forecasting that dairy prices would remain strong, if perhaps a little weaker than the record prices seen. In Rabobank's Q4 2013 report, the investment bank forecast that whole milk powder prices (the industry benchmark) would fall from approximately $5,000 per tonne (US dollars) to $4,300 per tonne by the end of

2014. One year later on from that forecast, whole milk powder prices had more than halved in price to $2,229 per tonne. Although the bank recognised the role that China played in driving demand, they made no mention that a slowdown in the rate of stockpiling by the Chinese was a potential downside risk. Indeed, they state, "We expect 2014 to bring a further increase in China's dairy purchases from the world market."[84] [85] [86]

The market for milk and other dairy products quickly turned from boom to bust. China purchased more milk than it needed and then, when it found itself awash with milk, pressure was placed on dairy exporters, such as those in New Zealand, to bear the pain of adjustment, rather than China's own domestic dairy industry.

NZ$10,000 (equivalent to US7,300 or £5,700) per cow – is the amount of debt that New Zealand's farmers had at one point, equivalent to approximately 20% of the country's GDP. The decline in dairy prices caused a fall in the value of dairy cows, which meant that farmers struggling to make debt repayments could not simply sell their animals to pay back the loans. The situation was so bad for many farming communities that some dairy farmers resorted to suicide, seeing no other way out from the collapse in milk prices and the impact on their incomes.[87]

"A lot of farmers are asking how the hell did we get into this mess?" says Chris Lewis, a farm owner and president of the Federated Farmers' Waikato division. "This is the season when many people will have to decide whether to stay in dairy or get out." The pain was felt across an industry that stretches from the Pacific to the EU and North America and employs millions. The pain forced many farms to restructure, to reduce their costs and to seek to merge with other farms in an effort to capture economies of scale when demand eventually recovers.[88]

In the US, dairy farmers' big bet on global demand for milk also soured badly. Herds expanded to a 20 year high just as demand from China and other emerging economies faltered, while the sharp drop in the price of grains also pushed down the value of meat. Commodity markets like dairy are prone to booms and busts because of the long lead time to ramp up supply. But just as it takes time to increase supply, it can't just be stopped once demand falters. "You can't turn the cows off," said Ken Nobis, president of a dairy co-operative in Michigan.

The outlook for commodity prices and the power of the commodity forecasters and pundits is more than just of academic interest. To take the example here, milk is one product that almost all of us take for granted and consume in some form or another (even if skimmed of fat and lactose). It also taps into our primal fears about the supply of food and nourishment for our children and the sustainability of the countryside. Agricultural commodities are typically produced on a much smaller scale than energy or metal. While the examples of spectacularly bad decisions and bad management are much smaller, and by extension much harder to find, they do exist. However, the impact is likely to be felt on a much more personal level.

Back in New Zealand, Fonterra, a co-operative group founded in 2001, represents approximately 95% of the country's farmers and together process approximately 80% of its milk. At the start of each year, the group provides an opening forecast of the price it is willing to pay farmers for their milk for the upcoming season (forming part of an advanced payment that goes to farmers early in the year). According to Keith Woodford, an independent consultant to the New Zealand dairy industry and honorary professor of Agri-Food Systems at Lincoln University, the co-operative's ability to forecast milk prices is less than encouraging. In the six years since 2011/12, Fonterra's milk price forecast for the upcoming season has been out by almost 20%. Woodford believes that forecasts from Fonterra and other institutions, as well as farmers, need to be more aware of how unpredictable dairy prices are. "It is time for all commentators who provide estimates about forthcoming dairy prices to emphasise the uncertainties. I have been arguing for some years that all dairy price projections should have a specified range of prices associated with them."[89] [90]

New Zealand is reliant on a global commodity where the main customers are emerging economies. According to Woodford, farmers have little option at present to be able to add value to their product, which could then help insulate them from price volatility:

> Part of our New Zealand problem is that we are heavily reliant on WMP (Whole Milk Powder) which is only used in big quantities by developing countries. However, shifting across to more value-add price-stable products is going to be a long-term rather than a short-term journey.

And part of the problem is the seasonal nature of the dairy market in New Zealand. According to Woodford, "With our seasonal production, we remain at a disadvantage for many of these value-add products. Seasonal production means low overall utilisation of costly processing plants, high inventory costs, and also increasing scrutiny from buyers concerning older-aged product."

For now, at least, dairy farmers in New Zealand will continue to be vulnerable to boom and bust periods of high and low prices. The lesson of the past few years is that the dairy market is just as subject to the laws of supply and demand as other commodities, and not nearly as predictable as many pundits believe.

Minor metals

Some commodity markets are tiny in comparison to the more conventional markets like oil, copper and iron ore. Minor metals for example include tungsten, indium, rare earth metals (REM) as well as a multitude of others with complex, exotic names. Unlike larger commodity markets, these metals are typically mined on a small scale and/or their production is a by-product of other much larger mining deposits. Macro-forces like urbanisation, consumer adoption of technology and the decarbonisation of economies are bringing many of these minor metals to the fore, as business models are re-shaped around a more sustainable and circular form of economic growth. The opaqueness of these markets means that they are particularly prone to speculative excess. The apparent unpredictability of future technological innovations (just think how mobile phones have developed over the past ten years) creates a problem for mining executives trying to match supply of minerals with anticipated demand many years into the future. The allure of many of the mining companies operating in this area is that the pace of innovation and therefore our demand for minor metals (such as REMs, lithium and cobalt) could increase at a much far faster pace than those planning and building mines can supply.

Meanwhile, understanding the supply of these metals is difficult to say the least because it is often hidden behind a corporate or state veil of secrecy. This can be the case for many commodities, but particularly for those minor metals that are considered to be of high geopolitical importance. For example, when one private organisation dominates the market, as Companhia Brasileira de Metalurgia e Mineração (CBMM) does for niobium (~85% of global supply), critical market data is missing to outside investors. In addition, since most minor metals exist as by-products next to more established commodities such as copper, they don't necessarily respond neatly to the laws of supply and demand. For example, tellurium (a metal four times scarcer in the Earth's crust than gold) is nearly always found in copper mine waste. However, unless copper miners have supplies of easy to access tellurium-laden copper waste lying around, a higher price for tellurium doesn't provide enough incentive for copper producers to produce more of it. Due to the high cost of separating these minor metals from other commodities, prices often need to cross a certain threshold to encourage a new and more expensive method of production – this results in a kind of stepped cost curve, where supply only responds if prices rise sharply enough.

One person that is at the forefront of this trend is Chris Berry, founder of House Mountain Partners. Berry focuses on those minor metals that are essential to powering the economies of the future, those that enable the generation of renewable energy, its storage and its use in applications like electric vehicles. This list of metals includes lithium, cobalt and graphite, as well as much larger and more conventional commodities like copper and nickel that are also likely to be important. Founded in 2009, Berry set up House Mountain Partners as an independent research provider that can point to opportunities for value creation in those commodities, which despite their rise in prominence over the past few years, are still under followed and are a not very well understood niche.

When I interviewed Berry, he explained that the biggest challenge facing investors in minor metals like lithium, cobalt and graphite is that their supply chains are just so much more complex than more conventional commodities:

> These markets are characterized by opaque pricing structures and very demanding specifications from end users. It's not enough to just mine lithium and produce lithium hydroxide. A mining company needs to do this in addition to securing binding off-take agreements which specify price and quantity for a specific length of time. Each section of the supply chain (mining, chemical conversion, end uses such as batteries or aerospace) is an investment opportunity in and of itself.

As an investor, you also need to factor in what the potential substitutes are (if any) and whether, just like for producers, there is a particular price point at which manufacturers also say enough is enough, we need to look for substitutes or reduce the amount of this metal in our product. The rapidly evolving technological innovation in batteries, for example, makes this particularly challenging. Here's Berry again:

> The markets are small (lithium at 190,000 tpa, cobalt at 120,000 tpa, etc), pricing is opaque and can vary

widely, and as technology continues to evolve, it becomes difficult to accurately forecast demand as it could increase or decrease for certain metals. As an example, there is a big move among battery scientists to remove cobalt from various lithium ion chemistries. This has been accomplished at bench scale, but typically when you remove or substitute one raw material in an end use, you end up using more of another. As cobalt use decreases in certain lithium ion chemistries, more nickel is typically required. How this affects economics really needs to be examined on a case by case basis.

Berry admits, though, that forecasting the price of these minor metals is little better than guesswork, which can potentially have costly implications for investors who are taken in by the narrative of ever-rising prices:

> Stockpiles, recycling, scrap, new products, and geopolitical tumult are some of the main issues that need to be factored in when forecasting prices for metals and equities. While discounted cash flow models (DCFs) are a widely used tool to determine valuations, I happen to think they're almost totally useless for most resource equities. This is especially true for assets such as resource deposits that have no operating history and hence no history of revenue, cash flow generation, or operating income. There are just way too many assumptions being made to reliably forecast prices or asset valuations.

As we've seen throughout this book, people dislike the uncertainty of the future. They will all too easily latch onto a pundit that provides the "faux" certainty that prices will do this or that in the future, even though that same pundit can be biased in their forecast and be subject to very different underlying motives from what appears on the surface. Since the outlook for the price of a commodity is one of the main determining factors behind future earnings, and hence the share price of mining shares, there is an incentive for the mining company to present as optimistic outlook as possible. But do investors recognise the potential for bias in commodity price forecasts presented in company prospectuses? Berry isnt convinced:

> They say they do, but it's difficult not to get overly excited by a bullish scenario. We've all been guilty of this, as have I. Much of the value destruction we've seen in the metals space comes from overly optimistic pricing assessments in economic reports like preliminary economic assessments.
>
> When prices are high and rising, it's easy to get lulled into thinking that "it's different this time". Unfortunately, my study of 140 years of commodity cycle data would indicate otherwise. Mean reversion is as sure as death and taxes.

Berry has an important message for investors in minor metals, one that is just as relevant for understanding other commodity markets – it's not enough to just understand the economics and the markets:

> To fully understand a company prospectus or economic study such as a PEA [preliminary economic assessment], you need knowledge of several different disciplines including finance, geology, and chemistry. This means it is very difficult to read between the lines and understand the true potential and pitfalls of various projects.

I asked Berry for his favourite example of bad capital allocation based on rosy forecasts of future commodity price rises. He replied, "Unfortunately, there are a few to choose from. Molycorp stands out only for the company's ability to over promise and under deliver and destroy billions in shareholder value." So what was it about this mine in the state of California that went so wrong to represent one of the most notorious examples of a commodity "white elephant"?

In 2010, Molycorp sensed an opportunity to capitalise on the high prices for REMs that had resulted from the cut in Chinese exports. The company's Mountain Pass mine was expected to be America's flagship source for REMs. The economics of Mountain Pass were built on extraordinarily rosy expectations of future prices. The Molycorp share prospectus included an assessment of current and future demand and supply for REMs and the implication for prices. Even accounting for the Mountain Pass facility starting production, prices for many of the metals were forecast to rise by 20-50% between 2010 and 2014, with prices forecast to double through to 2030. Nowhere in the prospectus was there any mention of the downside risks to prices, except this one line caveat in the footnote to the price forecast table, "that there will be no major changes to China's rare earth strategy and no new application(s) that will have a material impact on demand."[91]

What concerns me looking at the prospectus, and should also have concerned any prospective investor at the time, is that there was no attempt to quantify the risks that the REMs market presented. No thought into whether substitute sources of REMs would be developed and no thought into whether the high prices would encourage manufacturers to substitute REMs with some other much cheaper product or at least reduce the amount they required.

Were investors emboldened by the stratospheric and parabolic price of REMs and the story that the demand for REMs would continue to grow sharply due to growth in demand from defence and the tech industry? Maybe. Did they think that China would continue to restrict supply indefinitely? Maybe. However, a cursory look at the history of other commodity markets should have given enough evidence to suggest that what goes up, inevitably goes down, eventually.

After REMs prices fell sharply post-2011, and due to the high level of investment required, Molycorp was eventually forced into bankruptcy. Investors in Molycorp were by no means the only suckers to fall for parabolic price increases as a trend. According to Berry, many other REM mining companies were using three year trailing averages to justify their expectations of future prices. These price expectations then enabled what should have been a marginal project to get a valuation of over a billion dollars, and enabled many funds to be raised.

To an extent, it's all about incentives, especially when it comes to early stage mining or exploration companies. In the early stages, running one of these companies is often more about salesmanship - convincing others to invest in your ideas - than geology. Executives spend all their time looking for financial resources, rather than those in the ground. And here there is the incentive to present the best possible story of how the future – prices, in particular – may pan out.

One final word from Berry on the dangers to investors: "Beware narratives of limitless demand and limited supply which is nonsense junior mining companies excel in propagating. Any supply shocks will usually be met by some combination of recycling, thrifting, or technological advancement which displaces these unique materials."

By now you can see why minor metals and the share price of those companies that mine them can quickly be subjected to speculative excess. If forecasts for oil, the most important commodity to the functioning of the global economy and the most widely traded commodity, can be out by approximately 30% over just a six month period, then what prospects are there for predicting the movement of thinly traded markets such as REMs, lithium and cobalt? So what is the downside to all this mal-investment? According to Berry, the impact is far greater than just losses to investors:

> Mis-allocated capital harms trust and ruins livelihoods. I can't think of a single institutional investor who will consider investing in rare earth element projects given the boom and bust of 2010 – 2012. With many metals prices range bound, it is a high risk, moderate reward business so you need to understand and consider various parts of energy metals supply chains as investment opportunities.

Petrochemical capacity in the US

Petrochemical prices are notoriously volatile. Sharp upswings in virgin plastic prices typically incentivise the building of lots more capacity, but because of long lead times this capacity may only come on-stream just as prices plummet. Then, as prices plunge the depths, there is little incentive to cut capacity as long as each plant can be cash positive – further perpetuating the volatile cycle.

One industry expert who has been at the heart of this business is Paul Hodges, chairman of International eChem and author of "Boom, Gloom and the New Normal". When I interviewed Hodges for this book he explained that the petrochemical industry is in a very challenging part of the supply chain, having to manage both short- and long-term interests:

> Business in the middle of the supply chain such as petrochemicals can be squeezed on both sides. You have to be a bit like the Roman god, Janus, looking both ways at once. Because you look upstream at oil markets and you look downstream to consumer markets. There is very little connection between the two. If consumer start to take off with an enormous amount of demand, that doesn't mean that the energy markets start producing a lot more. Equally if demand from the consumer is slow, that doesn't automatically mean that the energy market slows. They are working on different timescales – one years or decades, the other weeks or months by and large. So the petchem industry is inevitably the buffer.

Given this unenviable position, the sector has to try to anticipate what prices are going to do in order to try to stay ahead of the competition:

> And what makes it more volatile is that the margins, because you are in the middle you are getting squeezed by both of these. And what people do to try to get around that problem is they take a view on how prices are likely to move. If we are a plastics consumer, for example, sometime around the middle of April we ask ourselves will the price of oil go up or down. If prices are expected to rise, then everyone down the chain builds inventory in anticipation of higher prices. And what that does is it gives a very confusing picture of demand.

According to Hodges, even executives in the petrochemical industry don't spend their days looking at the minutiae of oil price forecasts. They take shortcuts, just like everyone else, assuming that if the oil price is high it must mean that demand is strong. But just because everyone is doing it, doesn't mean there isn't a better way. Arguably, they should have paid much closer attention to what oil price forecasts left out back in 2011 and certainly also as late as mid-2014.

Back in 2010-14, forecasts of high oil prices ($100 per barrel plus) continuing long into the future contributed to one of the largest mis-allocation of funds ever seen in the commodity industry. Oil and natural gas prices in the US have historically tracked each other based on relative energy values (oil has approximately six times the energy value of gas). Up until around 2008, any difference in relative values has been rapidly arbitraged away over a period of a few years or so. However, from 2008 the difference in relative values blew out to enormous proportions.

The breakdown in the close relationship between US natural gas prices and crude prices from 2007 incentivised large scale investments in petrochemical capacity built on the assumption that recent history would trump several decades. Natural gas prices would remain low, while oil prices would remain high, maintaining the margin for ethylene producers. Industry consultant, IHS estimates that $160bn of petrochemical investment was built on the basis of a long-standing shale gas price advantage being sustained.[92]

Taken in by the prospect of large margins, ethylene producers also forgot to think about where all this additional ethylene was going to be sold. For while supply was also increasing elsewhere in the world, particularly in places like China, the demand side of the equation was also evolving rapidly. According to Hodges, the nature of demand for products made from polyethylene and other plastics is changing as the population ages. Investors were also worried that many of these investments apparently proceeded without the security of signed off-take contracts. This also mirrors developments in the mining industry, where euphoria over the outlook for China was the key driver.

According to Hodges, the over expansion in ethylene capacity in the US is just yet another example of how investors and businesses can get taken in by extrapolating the recent past, long into the future:

> The end result of this is that people have wasted billions of dollars, tens of billions of dollars on new investments to provide more

> supply which is simply never going to be used. It's a repeat, if you remember of the final stages of the dot com bubble. People were laying fibre cable everywhere in the world, much of which was never used. On the scale of what's happening today, it's two part of bugger all. Because of what's happening in oil, vast amounts of investments have been made that will never be needed; economies have been completely upended and disrupted, which will have all sorts of major implications for their security further down the track. And consumers have paid an enormous price for something that they didn't need.

Although over investment inevitably leads to low prices, there is a case for arguing that this isn't all good news for consumers; for what consumers really want is stability at an affordable price. Hodges claims that:

> What makes life really hard is when the price becomes unaffordable, because then you start to do other things to get around that issue, you do more investment and so on. And secondly if you get unnecessary volatility, that has a cost in terms of running your supply chain and in terms of the consumer managing your household budget.

Hodges believes that over the time that he has been involved in commodity markets, the quality of knowledge has gone down because the quantity of information has gone up. "We use to talk about a value chain of data, knowledge and understanding. Nowadays that isn't thought necessary by many investment banks." He goes even further and argues, as I do that together investor greed and much of the mainstream financial news media have propagated a system where critical analysis is thought to be secondary to a good story:

> You've created a system where people who shout loudest attract the most attention, even though what their shouting about is something that requires quiet consideration. The way forward is quiet, balanced discussion. There are quite a few people around the world who think the same way, but unfortunately, common sense is not very common. The danger is that the more educated you are the more you will look down on common sense because you think that undermines your intellectual arrogance.

Are resources a curse?

In "Commodities: 50 Things You Really Need To Know", I discussed the concept of the "resource curse". The resource curse typically describes the apparent relationship between the increase in a country's exploitation of natural resources and a decline in the manufacturing or agricultural sector of an economy.

An abundance of natural resource wealth can also distort economies in a number of other ways. Private investment in other less exploitable/profitable sectors of the economy may stagnate, leaving the government and economy highly dependent on resource revenues. This may be okay when commodity prices are high, but if they decline or suffer high volatility, and the economy is reliant on one commodity, then the economy becomes very vulnerable.

The commodity bust since 2011 exposed deep-seated problems that were covered up during the boom, as governments and citizens expected the good times to carry on. Over-optimism about Chinese commodity demand caused unneeded investments to be made in many emerging economies that fed the commodity boom and political corruption that only led to even worse capital mis-allocation.[93]

> A further problem is the potentially corrosive effect of commodity production on political institutions. Many commodities incorporate rents (ie, excess profits derived from the fact that supply is usually limited in the short term). Given that many commodity producers are owned and managed by the government, it is in the state's interest to capture those rents, but corruption often follows when it does.

The danger is that once commodity prices fall it can leave economies dangerously exposed. Whole countries can become "white elephants".

Even the expectation of a resource boom can lead to some of the problems associated with the "resource curse", even if not a single mineral is actually extracted. Researchers from Oxford University found that the mere expectation of future natural resource booms in São Tomé e Príncipe and Madagascar led to "resource curse" effects, even though neither country actually experienced the expected boom. Both countries experienced significantly more volatile economic growth and eroded political governance.[94]

What role do unrealistic expectations have in aggravating the effects of the "resource curse"? Well, first the mere expectation of a commodity boom can increase corruption and can lead to a change in the allocation of public resources. Over-optimistic price expectations only make the necessary adjustment to public finances that bit more painful. Terry-Lynn Karl and Ian Gary from the Institute of Policy Studies asserted that "oil booms raise expectations and increase appetites for spending" and that, as a result, "governments dramatically increase public spending based on unrealistic revenue projections".[95]

Secondly, expectations of future resource revenues from commodities can cause economic effects, such as changes in the real exchange rate that adversely affect the manufacturing and service sectors. Richard Auty of Lancaster University pointed out that the neglect of non-resource sectors resulted "in part from over-optimistic expectations for both mineral prices and RBI [resource-based industry] output". Furthermore, unmatched expectations of higher personal incomes among the population can cause popular discontent and lead to societal conflicts. As Gisa Weszkalnys from the London School of Economics notes in reference to an oil boom, "occasionally, it is thought to be just the expectation of oil that causes the curse to happen".[96] [97]

Brazil

The highest profile country that has suffered the most since the commodity bust has been Brazil. Yet Brazil was the first letter of the moniker BRICs, popularised by Goldman Sachs to represent some of the major emerging economies of the early 2000s. Not long ago, Brazil stood as the leading example of how a developing nation could rise toward global prominence on the back of a China-driven commodity boom. As its economy surged, Brazil stormed the world stage – hosting a World Cup, demanding more say at the United Nations and blocking a US free-trade plan for the Americas and hosting the Olympics. Now Brazil is looking like a symbol of something else: resource-rich nations have a habit of ending their booms with spectacular busts.

Looking back, it is easy to understand the frenzy of optimism. If the biggest economic story this century was China's rise, Brazil was uniquely poised to benefit from it. Rich in iron ore, soybeans, beef and oil, Brazil was positioned as a supplier of many of the things that China desperately needed. Its annual trade with China soared from $2 billion in 2000 to $83 billion in 2013, supplanting the US as Brazil's largest trading partner.[98]

China's rise helped spur global investors to pour more than $1 trillion a year into emerging markets by 2011, a five-fold increase in a decade. Brazil was a leading destination. Its securities markets were more transparent than China's, therefore some investors bought Brazil as way to play China.

Jim O'Neil recognised the potential for problems in the first letter of BRICs in his book "The Growth Map":[99]

> These days I do worry that Brazil might be partially suffering from the so-called "Dutch disease" [so called after the Netherlands experienced a decline in its manufacturing sector after gas was discovered]. As a result of the country's richness in commodity wealth, and with its high interest rates, the currency might have risen too far too fast, and this may damage the manufacturing part of the

economy.

O'Neil went on to say:

> In mid-2011, Brazil possibly has the most overvalued currency of the BRIC's. In the long term, I remain extremely optimistic about Brazil, and its recent success after decades of economic failure, are grounds for great hope. In the shorter term, I suspect that the strength of the real will be problematical.

Commodity prices then began to decline in early 2011 and like the tide retreating from the shore left Brazil without its proverbial bathing gown. Brazil's economic decline is partly due to the fall in commodity prices, but partly due to the build up of liabilities and the mismanagement built on the premise that revenues from commodities would continue to rise and Brazil's economic growth would remain strong. In turn, this was used to justify the government's fiscal largess in terms of public spending commitments.

Brazil turned itself into an expensive place to do business. A complex tax system, over generous pensions, poor transport infrastructure, high wages relative to its competitors and pointless regulation. In dollar terms, movies and taxis in downtown São Paulo were more expensive than in New York. The country's intoxication with its commodity boom with China also helped to turbo-charge many other unhealthy practices. From corruption to bribery, the intoxication eventually claimed the head of Ms Rouseff, Brazil's president, accused of corruption and mismanagement.

Even resource companies most exposed to the country were in denial over the extent of the problem. "In the corporate world, you spend half your life making forecasts and the other half explaining why that forecast was wrong." That was Vale's ferrous-division director, José Carlos Martins, who in mid-2014 kept telling investors that iron ore prices would remain high even as they kept on falling.[100]

It's worth noting that while the Goldman Sachs paper from 2003, "Dreaming with BRICs: The Path to 2050", sets out the economic rationale for why the five members of the group are included, it does not include a single mention of the role that commodity prices could have in binding their relationship together. It also does not mention the risk that a fall in commodity prices could have on the performance of Brazil or any of the other countries, or the risk that resources could be mismanaged. Indeed as soon as Brazil and the other members of the BRICs became tainted, or at least lost some of their shine, the search was on for another group of even more emerging economies upon which the growth of the global economy and rising demand for commodities would be based.[101]

Brazil, according to an old joke is "…the country of the future—and always will be."

"Minegolia"

Another example of a country that rode on China's economic coattails was Mongolia. During the commodity super-cycle that peaked in 2011, Mongolia had an epic run. Stoked by a booming Chinese economy and brisk foreign direct investment flows, Mongolia was one of the fastest-growing economies in the decade that ended in 2015. Its economy clocked in with an average real GDP growth rate of 8%, while per capita income surged to about $4,000.

The country of roughly 3 million people is

blessed with abundant natural resources (estimated by the International Monetary Fund to be valued at somewhere between $1-$3 trillion in 2011), and so attracted billions of dollars in mining investment. According to The World Bank, Mongolia was "at the threshold of a major transformation driven by the exploitation of its vast mineral resources."[102]

It all went bad when China's growth throttled back from double-digit levels in 2011, just as the Mongolian government went on a debt-fuelled spending binge. Then, in August 2016, came the collapse of the currency, the tugrik. Construction groups, thought to have borrowed heavily from abroad and in particular from China, were now saddled with much higher debts with no way of paying them off.

The authorities were also stuck in a similar position, having borrowed heavily on the back of the boom in commodity prices. Foreign exchange reserves tumbled to $1.3 billion by mid-2016, a 23% decline from a year earlier. Steep salary cuts of up to 60% were forced on some staff on the state payroll. The debt-fuelled binge also extended to individual families and communities too, with workers borrowing heavily against their salaries and pensions and contributing to a boom in demand for upmarket foreign cars and other luxuries.

Although I have some sympathy for Marc Faber's point that investment manias are an integral part of capitalism, I would prefer my money is not on the line when an investment turns sour. In writing this book, I hope it is not your money either. Unfortunately, as night follows day these examples of capital misallocation from the dairy, minor metals and petrochemical industries and those economies most exposed to Chinese demand for commodities will not be the last. As an investor, you may not be totally dependent on the outlook for commodity prices. However, for many individuals, communities, and even whole countries their futures may turn decidedly bleak if commodity markets turn against them. It is especially important that policymakers recognise this risk. So how do you avoid being lumbered with a "white elephant"? The next chapter are my key recommendations that policymakers, company executives, investors and the financial media should heed for a less forecast error prone future.

Chapter 9: Recommendations

"Whenever you find yourself on the side of the majority, it is time to pause and reflect."

Mark Twain

"Instead of posing as prophets we must become the makers of our fate. We must learn to do things as best we can, and to look out for our mistakes."

Karl Popper

What can we as investors, governments, companies, institutions and the financial media do better? There isn't one simple thing that will change attitudes. Our innate fear and greed for the future are powerful emotions that can cause us to lose our sense of perspective when we are under pressure. Based on the research from this book, these are my seven recommendations: 1. firm up fuzzy forecasts and track them; 2. scenario plan instead; 3. do your own research; 4. better data; 5. smarter media consumption; 6. stop forecasting and 7. know the knowable. Each recommendation is discussed in detail in this chapter.

Recommendation 1: Firm up fuzzy forecasts and track them

What can the forecasting profession do differently? Well, like most things in life, change will only happen if you demand it. Sharp words about failed predictions are essentially forbidden where they are most needed. So for all the incentives pushing experts to pump up their predictions, there must be a countervailing incentive to tone it down. In reality, there is little accountability for predictions, and while big calls that go bad should damage the reputations of those who make them, they seldom do.

Given how pervasive and influential commodity price predictions are, there is a surprising lack of data into how accurate the forecasts have been and which forecasters have the best track record. According to Philip Tetlock and Dan Gardner – authors of "Superforecasting: The Art and Science of Prediction" – there is a lack of accountability when it comes to financial forecasts. "Every day, the news media deliver forecasts without reporting, or even asking, how good the forecasters who made the forecasts really are," say Tetlock and Gardner. They continue:[103]

> Every day, corporations and governments pay for forecasts that may be prescient or worthless or something in between. And every day, all of us – leaders of nations, corporate executives, investors and voters – make critical decisions on the basis of forecasts whose quality is unknown.

Governments, businesses, investors and individuals don't demand evidence of accuracy before deciding whether to accept and act on a prediction. Forecasts are routinely made but the results are almost never tracked. As noted earlier, prominent forecasters build reputations not because of their accuracy but because of their skill at telling a compelling story with conviction.

Predict if you want, and rely on predictions if you really need to, but keep a tally of the predictions. Although my review of oil price forecasts over the past ten years was relatively easy to carry out, many of the predictions that pundits make are much more difficult to gauge. Part of the problem is the fuzzy language in which many predictions are often expressed, making it difficult to tell if the forecast was right or wrong even after the event.

Karl Popper famously made the observation that the usefulness of a prediction was related to its potential for falsification. "It will rain in London in the future" is a statement that is 100% accurate, but useless when it comes to telling us which day we should carry an umbrella. A statement that it will rain at 10.30am tomorrow is much more useful; it will rain or it will not. If it doesn't, then we can examine what assumptions were used in the forecast that turned out to be false.

Forecasts are often expressed using ambiguous words like probable, possible and risk, for which there are no agreed definitions, making it impossible to score them afterward. The US Intelligence Community has famously struggled with the lack of precision in the meaning of words that are commonly used to express likelihood and chance since the 1960s. Sherman Kent, often described as the "father of intelligence analysis", was a CIA analyst that recognised the problem of using imprecise statements of uncertainty. Particularly, Kent was jolted by how policymakers interpreted the phrase "serious possibility" in a national estimate about the odds of a Soviet attack on Yugoslavia in 1951. After asking around, he found that some thought this meant a 20% chance of attack, while others ascribed an 80% chance to the phrase. Most people were somewhere in the middle.[104]

Remember, hits and misses don't come with labels. It's often a matter of perception whether a forecast is deemed to be a hit or a miss, which makes language important. The more ambiguous the wording is, the more a pundit's prediction can be stretched. And since we want hits, that's the direction in which things will tend to stretch. As Dan Gardener describes in his book "Future Babble":[105]

> When the notoriously vague Oracle of Delphi was asked by King Croesus of Lydia whether he should attack the Persian Empire, the oracle is said to have responded that if he did he would destroy a great empire. Encouraged, the king attacked and lost.

The same confusing probabilistic terminology are used by pundits, and are then often also used by many in the financial media to imply something is much more likely to happen than it actually is. We saw an example of that in a previous chapter when Goldman Sachs suggested that because of limited spare capacity oil prices "could lead to $150-$200 a barrel oil prices" – many in the financial media interpreted "Could" as "Will".

In other cases, relatively specific forecasts are matched with an unspecific time frame, which also makes it difficult to score them for accuracy. There is a maxim among professional analysts that cynically confirms the problem: "always predict a price, or a time frame, but never both". However, in recent years, some commodity market forecasters have been pushed to quantify their forecasts by making specific price predictions over specified time horizons. Many have also embraced uncertainty by offering forecasts in the form of a probability distribution, rather than a point estimate, which is a much more useful and realistic way to think about the future. Commodity market forecasters are catching up with weather forecasters and the US Intelligence Community in trying to estimate the likelihood of a whole range of outcomes, not just the central one.

Percentage forecasts are an important step forward, but the commodity market is still lagging behind in terms of measuring forecast accuracy after the event. The problem with percentage forecasts is working out whether they were accurate even in retrospect. Tetlock and Gardner call this problem "being on the wrong side of 'maybe'". To understand the problem, imagine a weather forecaster who says that tomorrow there is a 70% chance of rain. The forecast also implies there is a 30% chance it will not rain. If it doesn't rain, the forecast was not necessarily wrong in a statistical sense but it is still likely to be criticised by anyone concentrating on more than just the most likely outcomes.

Although assigning probabilities to particular scenarios is an improvement, it is far from being a panacea. It can give an impression of faux certainty, that all possible outcomes are knowable in advance and have been captured by the forecast. Known as "Knightian uncertainty", probabilities cannot be assigned to different outcomes because the existing distribution of possible outcomes is unknowable.[106]

The danger with faux certainty is that it might lead market participants to believe something is more likely than it actually is. Consumers of forecasts might think that all of the possible outcomes have been captured by the commodity forecaster and then act based on this supposed "evidence". Remember, pundits see uncertainty as something that threatens their reputation. Often forecasters will make assumptions in their models that lower the perception of the degree of uncertainty in future prices.

Again, the solution to firming up fuzzy

forecasts is to track performance over time. This would weed out those forecasters unable to capture the range of possible outcomes accurately and the over-confident from the accurate. Meteorologists pioneered the solution to the probability forecasting problem and the solution was published by Glenn Brier of the US Weather Bureau in 1950. Brier published a careful methodology for comparing a set of forecasts expressed as probability distributions with eventual outcomes, and scoring forecasters on a standard scale from zero (complete accuracy) to 2.0 (perfect inaccuracy). The most accurate forecaster is the one whose forecast probability distributions get closest to the distribution of actual out-turns over time. If a forecaster predicts there will be a 70% chance of rain, they should be correct approximately 70% of the time.[107]

Verifying accuracy is obviously much easier for weather forecasts, where thousands of fresh forecasts are issued every day and can be compared with thousands of outcomes. Verification is more difficult for subjects like commodity prices but, given how frequently prices are forecast, it is not impossible and would be highly desirable.

Brier scoring price forecasts could also bring important benefits for commodity markets. The aim would not be just to identify the most accurate forecasters, those most worth paying attention to, but improving the accuracy of all forecasts by subjecting them to rigorous analysis after the event. Weather forecasts have improved enormously over the last fifty years because they have been subjected to rigorous analysis. It is far less obvious that forecasts for commodity prices and other financial markets have become any better.

In "Black Box Thinking", Matthew Syed describes how the airline industry actively promotes the sharing of mistakes and failures in order to help propel the safety of the industry forward. Other professions are not so great at looking at past mistakes, learning from them and improving their processes and models to make the future better. Syed describes how psychotherapists gauge whether their treatments are effective, not by observing the patient with objective data over a long period of time, but by observing them in the clinic. As well as being prone to all kinds of biases, both from the patient and the psychotherapist, there is no feedback on the lasting impact of the treatment and hence no opportunity to learn – from success and from failure.[108]

There is no reason why learning from mistakes and failures should not be part of the job description of the analysts involved in commodity forecasting. Capturing data is not a problem (whether that be prices, futures market activity, etc), information on market events are well publicised (for example, changes in interest rates, currency movements or political instability). All it needs is a change in attitude.

A great example of learning from failure and, importantly, being very open and transparent about it comes courtesy of Michael Liebrich from Bloomberg New Energy Finance. Every January, Liebrich and his colleague, Chief Editor Angus McCrone, dust off their crystal balls and predict what the coming year will bring. Then, and this is where their approach is so refreshing, they revisit their predictions at the end of the year, mark their scores and highlight what took them by surprise. Here is an extract from their review of their ten predictions for 2016, in which they discussed how well they did in their second forecast of 2016 in which they predicted the outlook for commodity prices over the year:[109]

FOSSIL FUEL PRICES BACK FROM THE ABYSS:

In January, we pointed out: "The new game among oil analysts (remember them – they're the folks who were on your TV screens two years ago predicting $200 oil prices) is to predict new oil price lows at $20 or even $10 per barrel."

We refused to play the game of predicting the bottom of the market, saying instead that we expected "oil and coal prices to bottom out during 2016 and end the year somewhat higher than they are now." As it turns out, by pure luck, we timed the bottom of the fossil fuel market almost to the day. On January 18, the day our forecast was published, Brent crude opened at $28.73 amid a sea of pessimistic market views. It fell for just two more days, hit its low for the year of $27.10 on January 20, and then turned, climbing steadily for the rest of the year – helped during December by the stunning reversal of OPEC's two-year-old open-tap policy. The ARA steam coal contract took a little longer to hit bottom, but that came on February 17, some $1.20 below where it was when I made the prediction, before rallying strongly to the $78-a-tonne area now."

SCORE: 10/10

Note their reference to the luck they had in

timing the market bottom. You could argue that they got the direction right and that anyone can do that with a coin flip. A score of 10 out of 10 is a bit of a big pat on the back, right? Well, yes, but my point is that they are not hiding their luck or pretending that they have some innate ability or foresight that others do not possess. And that's kind of refreshing to see.

Recommendation 2: Scenario plan instead

There is an alternative to forecasting and that's to scenario plan instead. Rather than making forecasts, scenario planning involves sketching out different possibilities and bringing together people with different perspectives to work through the details. The end result should be several plausible, internally consistent and emotionally compelling stories about the future. The scenarios will highlight hidden connections and make distant consequences seem real. Importantly, though, the scenarios should also contradict each other.

Since scenarios are persuasive stories, they can help us face up to uncomfortable prospects and think clearly about possibilities we would rather ignore. And because scenarios contradict each other, they force us to acknowledge that, in the end, we cannot actually see into the future. As a result, we move from a sterile question to a fertile one – from "What will happen?" to "What will we do if it does?"

Arguably, what is most important to commodity producers and consumers is not having a forecast of future commodity prices but understanding the risk that prices will go to extreme levels, either high or low, during a particular period, and the impact this could have and what mitigating actions should be taken. If you are planning on building a petrochemical plant, deciding to plant a certain crop one year rather than another, whether to leave your energy needs unhedged or something else, the key question is to ask "What is the worst that can happen and what would we do about it?", and on the flipside, "What is the best that can happen?" Not just the most recent example of what constitutes "the best" or "the worst", but a more extreme version.

Scenario planning is no silver bullet though. Scenario planning – and any other sort of imaginative speculation about the future – can indeed push us out of the rut of recency bias. However, it can also shove us right over to the other extreme, where we greatly overestimate the likelihood of change. First, by its very nature scenario planning involves coming up with colourful scenarios of the future, draped in lots of description about how this outcome could come about and plenty of other supporting bits and pieces, much of which might or might not be realistic. Second, a narrative (A might lead to B, which could then lead to C and D happening) of how things could unfold in the future is very compelling, but can also lead the producer and consumer of that narrative to think that it is much more likely to occur than it actually is.

A well-done forecast or scenario plan identifies the possible scenarios, specifies key variables, shows the range of errors and focuses thinking for both the analyst and the reader, making them question their own views. This kind of long-term thinking is a personal favourite of mine. Not because of its forecasting prowess. No, looking several decades into the future is fraught with difficulties and will be wrong. But knowing what we know about human behaviour, it can be a useful way of challenging your mind to think through how the future could evolve.

The danger with scenarios, however, is that once they out in the public domain someone misinterprets a scenario as being a forecast. In mid-2017, the International Energy Agency (IEA) was on the hook. Many commentators took to social media to show, in their words, how bad the IEA's "predictions" of photovoltaic (PV) capacity had been. Many drew the connection that if the IEA had been so slow to predict PV capacity growth, then the IEA, and others, could similarly be underestimating the potential growth in electric vehicles. The IEA responded by arguing that:[110]

> The projections in the New Policies Scenario signal to policy-makers and other stakeholders the direction in which today's policy ambitions are likely to take the energy sector. This does not, however, make this scenario a forecast – a point that needs constantly to be kept in mind.

The IEA didn't help itself by frequently using the word "projections" in its analysis. Predictions and forecasts are far more marketable, if you are in the business of selling people advice. But that isn't what scenarios are meant to do.

The possibilities are endless. Just remember, a scenario is not a forecast.

Recommendation 3: Do your own research

New EU rules, set to come into force in 2018, will force asset managers to pay directly for research. Mifid II, formally known as the second Markets in Financial Instruments

Directive, is widely regarded as one of the most complex sets of financial rules to be introduced in response to the 2008 financial crisis. EU regulators became concerned that trading costs (which tend to be passed on to asset managers' clients) were inflated to include the cost of providing "free" research reports. The assumption being that investors had no idea they were inadvertently picking up the bill, while asset managers were failing to ensure they were getting value for money for their clients.

Research was frequently used as marketing fodder, raising the profile of the investment bank among current and potential new clients. Once these regulations are introduced, the incentive to appear on financial TV networks peddling their research will be much lower, or at least will only be open to those that can justify the expense. It will, in turn, open up the market to other alternative providers of research - independent research providers and consultants without an interest in the underlying market, and so outside of the Mifid II regulations. It will also mean that investors will need to do more of their own research, and with that comes a demand for a deeper understanding of commodities and commodity markets.

Ultimately, these rules could mean that commodity markets are not as liquid as they have been in the past, as investor interest diminishes. This could mean that markets are more volatile, and perhaps ultimately less efficient in incorporating information and market insight into the price. This will open up new opportunities to those able to spot them, which in turn means the demand for fresh insight is likely to grow.

One of the best ways to really understand a

market is to do your own research. This doesn't need to be an exhaustive study. You can do worse than picking up a long-term chart for a particular commodity and looking for the biggest spike or slump. Then ask yourself what happened there, what could those in the market have known at the time that the risk of a dramatic change in price was looming?

In the book "Market Wizards", legendary investor Jim Rogers highlights the great bull run in cotton in 1861, when the price of cotton went up from 0.5 cents per lb to 105 cents per lb, as an excellent example of a historical chart pattern worthy of studying. Of course, the risk that you should be wary of is hindsight bias – the risk that the spike in prices looks far more predictable with the benefit of over 150 years of knowledge. Yet the exercise still stands as a good one. And once you've done one, look at another. What were the differences? What were the similarities?[111]

We're so used to outsourcing our thinking to others that we've forgotten what it's like to really understand something from all perspectives. We've forgotten just how much work that takes. The path of least resistance, however, is just a click away. Reading headlines and skimming the news seems harmless, but it is harmful because it makes us over-confident. It's better to remember a simple trick: anything you're getting easily through Google or Twitter is likely to be widely known and should not be given undue weight.

Doubt is needed as an antidote to this. In Svend Brinkmann's excellent book "Stand Firm: Resisting the Self-Improvement Craze", Brinkmann rages against the craze for certainty that modern life demands and suggests that doubt is not just a luxury, but a necessary skill that we all should start to develop:[112]

> In essence, certainty is necessarily dogmatic, whereas doubt has an important ethical value. How do I figure that out? Well, certainty's "I know" easily leads to blindness – especially when you know that it's best to say yes. Doubt on the other hand leads to openness, to other ways of acting and new understandings of the world. If I know, I don't need to listen. But if I'm in doubt, other people's perspectives are endowed with greater meaning.

An understanding of economic history is the most important attribute to understanding the future. When I went to university there was a big focus on the use of econometrics in understanding the future. Statistics has its place, and I would definitely recommend some training in basic methods, but if I could go back and do something different, it would be to study more economic history.

Forecasts, and the research underpinning it needs to be evidence based. Generalisations such as this a particular chart pattern is 'bullish' or that an expected change in the fundamentals supports lower prices is not enough. As Brett Steenbarger, author of The Psychology of Trading highlights, "Evidence takes the con out of our investment confidence." Understanding the history of commodity markets, in the context of complex systems is the first step to improving your own research, and holding others work to account.[113]

Recommendation 4: Better data

I've highlighted the powerful impact that commodity price predictions can have on the future path of communities and, indeed, whole economies. But what can policymakers do to ensure that their economies and industries are anti-fragile and so less prone to booms and busts?

Better data on commodity demand and supply outside of the US must be the priority if policymakers want energy and other commodity markets to operate more smoothly. The activities of large commodity producers are particularly opaque. Better data on consumption in fast growing emerging economies will also help to give a more accurate assessment of demand prospects.

Some private companies and often large institutional investors deploy people to count cocoa stocks in the Ivory Coast, use infrared cameras to monitor oil levels in storage tanks in the US or set up cameras to film coal stocks at Japanese power stations. All are set to determine the inventory fluctuations and price discrepancies through which they and their clients can profit. This kind of inside edge is outside of the scope for all but the wealthiest people. Nevertheless, some participants in the commodity markets are fighting back. Using a combination of technology, crowd sourcing and social media, they are beginning to change things for the better.

Samir Madani, a consumer electronics entrepreneur, saw an opportunity to combine real time data with his passion for oil markets. Traditionally, oil researchers and forecasters would talk about their expectations for supply and demand. However, without knowing how much is being exported and how much is going into storage, the overall supply and demand estimates are of limited use. In 2017, Madani launched the not-for-profit website *Tanker Trackers* to help increase market transparency by combining crowd-sourced data on crude tanker movements and official data published by government agencies. "I love real-time data and felt that the average Joe had no insight into what's happening out at sea," Madani told me as he outlined his vision of how he could help disrupt the market to the benefit of "ordinary" traders:

> Two-thirds of the world's oil is transported by sea and instead of hearing what crystal-ball-polishers think the price of oil would be end of the year due to supply vs demand, I felt that I could do something about it.

It's here where crowd-sourced information on tanker loadings can help increase market transparency, hopefully allowing traders and physical market participants to make better decisions. For example, knowing that one week there was an unusually large spike in tanker loadings in Saudi Arabia destined for the US means that a trader can deduce that in approximately 45 days time there could be a big jump in crude inventories in the US.

Whichever way, the pursuit of better and more open data is likely to reduce uncertainty in commodity markets and potentially reduce price volatility too. Robert McNally, founder and president of energy consulting firm The Rapidan Group and the author of the book "Crude Volatility", believes that much more should be done to force or incentivise the energy industry to become more transparent (the same arguments are just as valid for other commodity markets):[114]

> The oil market is turbulent enough, patchy and incomplete data make the problem worse. Energy data reporting should be lawfully compelled, timely

and comprehensive. Upstream governments should require industry to disclose and validate field-by-field production and reserve data. Doing so would reduce surprises, manic hoarding, and price volatility. Downstream, figures for production, storage, net trade, and refining stocks and flows should be comprehensively reported, enabling much better implied demand estimates.

At the same time, individual traders and investors face an uphill struggle as the spread of information accelerates. Data and news no longer has to be read and processed by humans. Bots are absorbing this information automatically and handing it to programs to make trading decisions. Individual algorithms react to what others do, with decisions made on the sort of timescales that humans can never fully supervise. This can lead to dramatic and unexpected behaviour that may result in much higher price volatility, at least over very short time periods.

Recommendation 5: Smarter media consumption

TV financial media is designed to entertain you, not necessarily to enlighten you with insight that will make you better at making the right financial decisions. Like any form of entertainment, financial TV is designed as an assault on your senses, with all manner of irrelevant information in which to overwhelm our cognitive resources. This is made worse because financial TV enshrines forecasting, and those that provide them, at the centre of its coverage. Remember, truth is harder to sell than fear.

The question then becomes, is there anything

better?

The move away from an information system based around vertical axes of trust (ie, conventional research and investment institutions), to one predicated on horizontal axes of trust (ie, Twitter and other forms of social media), has important implications for commodity and other financial markets. Although you could argue that social media (whether that takes the form of blogging or updates on networks like Twitter) democratises the supply of information, commentary and forecasts, it also forces the consumer of that information to swim through an ever increasing flood of viewpoints and commentary in order to weed out the gems. In turn, it leaves them open to the risk of information overload and of being overly responsive to the latest market updates.

In research published by Oxford University, entitled "Social Media, News Media and the Stock Market", researchers found that the most talked about stocks on social media exhibited more volatility than those that did not. Although the research didn't specifically look at commodity futures, it would not take too much of a stretch to imagine a similar impact here.[115]

Despite the risks of information overload, maintaining a diverse set of information and views is likely to help raise returns for both traders and investors. Two academics at the MIT media lab in Boston – Sandy Pentland and Yaniv Altshuler – have been crunching vast quantities of computer data to track what happens to commodity and foreign exchange traders who are plugged into social media, such as Twitter. The MIT research suggests that investors do not perform as well when they are isolated from social groups. The image of a brilliant, maverick trader sitting alone and shunning conversation to order to make winning individual trades is wrong. However, neither do traders outperform when they are embedded too deeply in any single market group, be that the gold bug community, oil market watchers or enthusiasts for any other commodity market. Instead, the best returns occur when investors are plugged into diverse social groups that enable them to collide with information from multiple networks. In the social media world, as in real life, it pays to hover on the edge of cliques – but not get slavishly sucked into just one.[116]

Just as there is a danger in blindly following forecasts from renowned institutions, the MIT researchers argue that social effects are so strong that they sometimes over-ride individual's rational assumptions. Individual traders are often prone to much riskier behaviour when following their peers, and are much more likely to overreact when their peers are doing so and market uncertainty is high. All of the commodity traders in the world (whether you are a physical buyer or seller or just speculate on the price of commodity futures) are organised into networks of friends, colleagues, contacts and others who are all sources of information and opinion and therefore influence. According to the concept of herding and imitation, commodity traders tend to imitate the opinions of their "neighbours" in their network, not contradict them. Social media may make this effect even stronger.

Samir Madani is also the founder of the hashtag #OOTT. The Organization of Oil Trading Tweeters (#OOTT) has grown to become a go-to place for top journalists, editors, traders, researchers and investors wanting to read the latest news and developments affecting global oil markets. I asked Madani if, as the #OOTT hashtag expands, there is the potential for group-think to develop and will it just mean that it becomes harder to separate the signal from the noise? He replied:

> Actually, it's quite funny because it's VERY easy to spot what positions people are holding for the day (long/short) by the content they tweet out. The most unbiased folks are the ones that are not trading on that day. What's nice, however, is that there is no leniency to either as people swap sides all the time, so it balances out. I can find you just as many bulls as I can find bears. As co-founder of the #OOTT, I want to make sure that all news is presented, regardless if it's bearish or bullish. It's all about the facts, because winds shift very quickly in this game, and you'd want to know why!"

Oil is certainly the commodity market, perhaps along with gold, that gets the most attention from investors, but the impact of social media is far more widespread. The relatively private bulletin boards where the future of this or that commodity and the companies that produce them is still there; however, now you only need to search for a particular commodity or company and you can get a constant stream of unfiltered news and opinion. As with #OOTT, the trick is to spend enough time understanding each person's agenda and track record in order to filter out the noise.

In Chapter 4 I introduced the concept of reflexivity and how false hoods (ie, convincing narratives) can feed on themselves to take commodity markets well away from where the price should be. The occurrence of false trends is only likely to rise as global information and interpretation flow increases and narratives become more uniformed and accordant. Nassim Taleb put it well when he said:[117]

> The mind can be a wonderful tool for self-delusion – it was not designed to deal with complexity and nonlinear uncertainties. Counter to the common discourse, more information means more delusions: our detection of false patterns is growing faster and faster as a side effect of modernity and the information age: there is this mismatch between the messy randomness of the information-rich current world with its complex interactions and our intuitions of events, derived in a simpler ancestral habitat. Our mental architecture is at an increased mismatch with the world in which we live.

As information flows increase, it is now more important than ever to combine that with insight and knowledge. The commodity trader or investor of the future will find both on social networks. To this end, social media is something of a double-edged sword. According to Chris Berry:

> Most investors don't have an adequate foundation of the multiple skills necessary to ask the right questions or interpret the answers. As a result, people end up in chat rooms making all sorts of claims. One of the best things investors can do is stay out of chat rooms.

So what should you do? According to Tadas

Viskanta, author of "Abnormal Returns: Winning Strategies From the Frontiers of the Investment Blogosphere", you basically have two options, "The first is to simply eliminate, or at least dramatically cut back on news consumption... The other option is to try and consume media in a smarter, more focused way." If you as an investor, trader or producer or consumer of commodities have a time frame of more than several months, then there is a case for arguing that a media diet will help you. Nassim Taleb writes in his book, "Fooled by Randomness" that "the problem with information is not that it is diverting and generally useless, but that it is toxic." On the other hand, as the success of most other diets testifies a media diet may not be all that successful either if it means you become less able to sift the wheat from the shaft.[118]

And what about consuming media in a smarter, more focused way? There are two key aspects to this. The first is to focus on the best aggregators of information that are relevant to you. While this may result in you missing some bits of information, a competent aggregator of information should only highlight the information that is most relevant. Tadas Viskanta notes the value of following blogs, and here the market does a good job of working out who you should follow: "To a certain degree, the blogosphere is a meritocracy, an imperfect one for sure, but a meritocracy nonetheless. In general, the blogs that are consistently updated will find a growing readership."

The final key aspect of consuming media more effectively is to be multi-disciplined and read widely. According to Oaktree Capital's Howard Marks, "in order to be successful, an investor has to understand not just finance, accounting and economics, but also psychology." That's not just understanding the psychology of the market, but your psychology and also the psychology of the pundits and their inherent biases. I would also add geology and an understanding of technological disruption to Marks' "successful investor" list, and Chris Berry agrees:

> Understanding commodity market economics is a good and important start. On the metals side, an understanding of basic geology is also helpful. I also think an understanding of what disruptive innovation is and how it can affect various industries is important.

Recommendation 6: Stop forecasting

Why are we interested in the set path of a commodity over the next quarter, next year or next decade? Compare this to our personal lives – we are much more interested in understanding the major forks in the road ahead, things like love, health or work. As Didier Sornette highlights:[119]

> ...predicting the detailed evolution of complex systems has no real value, and the fact that we are taught that it is out of reach from a fundamental point of view does not exclude the more interesting possibility of predicting phases of evolutions of complex systems that really count, like the extreme events.

Two key observations can be made about the behaviour of commodity markets. First, no one really knows what events are going to transpire and, second, no one knows what the markets' reactions to those events will be. What was initially thought to be bullish for the price of a commodity one week might be bearish for that same commodity the next week.

Likewise, a focus on always being right about predictions demonstrates a fundamental misunderstanding of the point behind investing, trading and trying to achieve the best deal for the commodities you are buying or selling. As Tadas Viskanta notes:

> Traders need to recognise that that a large percentage, maybe even more than 50% of their trades, are going to fail. Traders can sometimes get hung up on the idea that they need to profit from most if not all of their trades. The fact of the matter is that being right is only part of what it takes to succeed in trading... All that really matters for traders is making profits and generating those profits with a reasonable amount of risk.

So what can be done to avoid these problems? The first and most obvious solution is to stop relying upon pointless forecasts. Second, we should redirect our efforts away from forecasting actual numbers. Having armies of analysts and economists all forecasting is a complete waste of time. There is a good reason we call analysts "analysts" and not "forecasters" – they are meant to analyse and not guess the unknowable future. They would be better utilised in analysing the present and understanding what that could mean for the future, rather than coming up with spurious anchors for investors to cling to. Anchors are a minefield for forecasters, and they do the consumer of forecasts no good either.

Finally, another issue largely overlooked in

understanding the cons of trying to forecast the market is the issue of costs. This doesn't just cover the financial cost of buying forecasts and research. Nor does it just include the potential risk that investors and physical participants in commodity markets potentially take because of following predictions. There is also the opportunity cost. The time and effort spent in trying to become better at predicting commodity markets, in trying to time the market better and in accessing more and more real time data and analysis has a cost, which by definition comes at the expense of other potentially more productive activities.

Recommendation 7: Know the knowable

History is a guide to how things will turn out in the future, but nothing more. Indeed, the accelerating pace of technological change may mean that the old cycles begin to play out much more rapidly in the future. According to hedge fund manager Howard Marks, that may make the job of the macroeconomic forecaster much more challenging in the future and one where an understanding of how technology usurps the existing cycles much more valuable:[120]

> I realised recently that in my early decades in the investment business, change came so slowly that people tended to think of the environment as a fixed context in which cycles played out regularly and dependably. But starting about twenty years ago – keyed primarily by the acceleration in technological change – things began to change so rapidly that the fixed backdrop view may no longer be applicable.
>
> Now forces like technological

developments, disruption, demographic change, political instability and media trends give rise to an ever-changing environment, as well as to cycles that no longer necessarily resemble those of the past. That makes the job of those who dare to predict macro more challenging than ever.

There could of course be a contradiction in Marks' prediction of the challenges involved in prediction. As can be heard almost any time someone frets about the future, there is the issue of hindsight bias. Someone says, "Things are uncertain, not like it was in the past." The first part of that statement is accurate; the second is not. The future is always uncertain, whether it is the future we face right now or the future that people faced a century ago.

I'll allow a bit of hindsight bias through this time – just for the sake of argument. If Marks is correct, then how should commodity traders and investors, as well as physical buyers and sellers, react to this new market? Well, when change is both inevitable and gaining speed, a person's ability to adapt to the market environment based on what can be observed here, right now, in the present is far more valuable than trying to predict the future. If Marks is right, then the changes we are seeing in society and business effectively mean that evolution is accelerating. Evolution and those best able to take advantage of commodity market trends both favour those individuals and organisations that can adapt the fastest and most effectively to that accelerated change.

Believing that we know and understand where we are now can lead us into the temptation that we can then extrapolate this to the future. For the successful, a delicate balancing act is required to guard against this inherent demand in our psyche and from others around us. According to Marks:

> We can't predict, but we can prepare... the key to dealing with the future lies in knowing where you are, even if you can't know precisely where you're going. Knowing where you are in a cycle and what that implies for the future is very different from predicting the timing, extent and shape of the next cyclical move.

The advice for traders and investors is that instead of attempting to second guess the future direction of economies and markets, devote yourself to specialised research in market niches. These are the inefficient markets in which it is possible to gain a "knowledge advantage" through the expenditure of time and effort. In the world of commodities this might include energy metals – like lithium, cobalt and uranium – that are hidden from view to the casual observer, but for which the evidence is there if you only care to look.

Try to know the knowable.

Chapter 10: Conclusion

We all secretly like to have clarity on the future. What will I be doing? Will my business be safe? What about my investments, my family? The problem becomes when we tie ourselves too closely to a forecast, believing the future will turn out as the pundits foretell.

This books preface began with a true story – a serious health scare in China that shocked authorities into action. Instead of relying on the tainted domestic milk, they sourced milk that could be trusted from overseas. Dairy farmers in New Zealand and many other countries around the world went into expansion mode, looking to cash in on the boom in Chinese demand and the expectations (a view reinforced by pundits and forecasters) that China was at the start of a long-term boom in dairy demand.

From the rural idyll of farming in New Zealand, the industrial heartland of petrochemical facilities in the US, to the Moon-like features of the mines of Canada, each has relied on predictions of the future to get to where they are today. However, bad forecasts that prop up bad investments are costly. They harm trust and ruin livelihoods. The example of the New Zealand dairy farmers, and the fallout from other ill-timed commodity market investments, demonstrates that it is now time for a different approach.

The experience of Brazil, Mongolia and other countries that are heavily dependent on the export of raw materials is that expectations matter. Forecasts matter. Whole countries have gone through turmoil on just the anticipation of a resource boom, even if they never actually get to see the benefits.

Commodity forecasts are typically not very

good. My analysis of oil price forecasts over a ten year period, where pundits were asked to look forward just six months out, revealed that they are typically out by almost 30%. If this is as good as it gets in the most liquid, most important commodity market in the world, then how does anyone stand a chance in other commodity markets?

Other research has found that the best predictor of the price is not some fancy model that takes account of demand and supply projections, nor the commodity futures curve that many commentators believe represents a kind of crowd-sourced view of price expectations. It's not even the exchange rate of commodity producing countries or technical analysis. As basic as it seems, the evidence suggests that the best predictor of the price in the future is... the current price. No self-respecting pundit would ever start forecasting the future price based on that nugget of insight, would they? At least not stating that was their rationale.

As the great investor Warren Buffet said, "Forecasts usually tell us more of the forecaster than the future." Just as investors, traders and buyers and sellers of commodities are biased, commodity price forecasters and pundits are biased too. Forecasters are too busy looking in the rear view mirror and looking across at their competitors to provide an unbiased forecast of the future. What they need is an incentive to get things right.

The price of a commodity is just not predictable on a consistent basis. The only thing that can be said with absolute certainty is that commodity prices will continue to defy the expectations of the experts. Only when experts stop pretending that they can predict the unpredictable will their credibility return. The expert may forget about their prediction failure due to hindsight bias, but the public can now easily fact check the record of the pundit. This reality will not change.

Investors need to be constantly reminded of their ability to check a pundit's record. Otherwise, it will be very easy to fall into the trap yet again. For those just too lazy to bother tracking the record of a pundit or an institution, then they will be easily swayed by their soothsaying words. In short, there will always be demand for pundits and their predictions of commodity prices, other financial asset prices and whatever else. But, let's at least start holding them to account.

Perhaps the most important lesson is that we spend too much energy trying to foretell the future. Yet we spend too little time trying to be resilient to whatever happens, and so not considering the risks that could affect our investments and businesses. Commodity producers and consumers must adapt to prices as they find them. Flexibility and the ability to survive through the price cycle are more important to producers and consumers than flaky forecasts about where prices are going over the next three, five or ten years. Meanwhile, as investors, we do not spend enough energy positioning our portfolios to take advantage of extreme scenarios becoming the default.

This book has to be a signal for change. I have included a number of recommendations on how the industry can improve. Keeping score of how well commodity price predictions turn out will certainly help. After all, if billions of dollars of investments are based on these predictions, the least anyone can do is verify how accurate they are. Firming up fuzzy forecasts needs to happen in order to allow the consumers of forecasts to verify commodity price predictions.

Ultimately, though, forecasts will only become more accurate and the nature of the pundit industry will only change if you demand it to. If you don't question the forecasts present in company prospectuses; if you don't question the biases that pundits are prone to; if you don't question their logic using the analysis of the economic, political and other drivers outlined in this book, then nothing will change.

Demand forecasts if you have to, but please demand better forecasts.

[1] Agricultural Export Restrictions and the WTO: What Options do Policy-Makers Have for Promoting Food Security? Issue Paper No 50. By Giovanni Anania, University of Calabria, Italy. (November 2013). *International Centre for Trade and Sustainable Development (ICTSD)*.
https://www.ictsd.org/downloads/2013/11/agricultural-export-restrictions-and-the-wto-what-options-do-policy-makers.pdf

[2] Outstanding Issues in the Analysis of Inflation, by Chairman Ben Bernanke. (9th June, 2008). *At the Federal Reserve Bank of Boston's 53rd Annual Economic Conference*.
https://www.federalreserve.gov/newsevents/speech/bernanke20080609a.htm

[3] Monthly Bulletin. (December 2014). *European Central Bank (ECB)*.
http://www.ecb.europa.eu/pub/pdf/other/mb201412_focus03.en.pdf?cbd4c6a71e2fcfdcd36c042c8181cef3

[4] Navarro's trade comments should be dollar-positive, by Barbara Rockefeller. (7th March 2017). *FX Street*. https://www.fxstreet.com/analysis/navarros-trade-comments-should-be-dollar-positive-201703071401

[5] "Future Babble: Why Expert Predictions Fail - and Why We Believe Them Anyway", Dan Gardner. (2011). Virgin Books

[6] WSJ Economic Forecasting Survey
http://projects.wsj.com/econforecast/#ind=oilprices&r=6&e=99

[7] The author recognises that he may be subject to the survivorship bias here, i.e. that some forecasters have dropped out of the sample if their firm was taken over/closed.

[8] "The Most Important Thing: Uncommon Sense for the Thoughtful Investor", Howard Marks. (2011). Columbia Business School Publishing

[9] Superstar CEOs, by Ulrike Malmendier & Geoffrey Tate. *The Quarterly Journal of Economics*, Volume 124, Issue 4, 1 November 2009, Pages 1593–1638, https://doi.org/10.1162/qjec.2009.124.4.1593

[10] The dangers of mixing forecasts and forward. (30th March 2015). *Timera Energy*. http://www.timera-energy.com/the-dangers-of-mixing-forecasts-and-forward-curves/

[11] The Predictive Content of Commodity Futures, by Menzie D. Chinn and Olivier Coibion. *Journal of Futures Markets*. (January 2013).
http://www.nber.org/papers/w15830

[12] The Growth of Nations, by Mankiw NG. (1995). *Brookings Papers on Economic Activity*.
http://scholar.harvard.edu/files/mankiw/files/growth_of_nations.pdf?m=1360042101

[13] Commodity Prices, Commodity Currencies, and Global Economic Developments: Working Paper 15743, by Jan J. J. Groen and Paolo A. Pesenti.

National Bureau of Economic Research. http://www.nber.org/papers/w15743

[14] A conclusion supported by other researchers. Real-time forecasts of the real price of oil, by Baumeister, C and Kilian, L. (2011). CEPR Discussion Paper No. 8414.
http://www.cirano.qc.ca/conferences/public/pdf/realtime2011/10-Kilian_Pres.pdf

[15] The Price of Oil in 2015, by Jim O'Neil. (7th January 2015). *Project Syndicate.* https://www.project-syndicate.org/commentary/price-of-oil-in-2015-by-jim-o-neill-2015-01?barrier=true

[16] LNG Seen Overtaking Iron Ore as Australia's Main Export Driver, by James Paton. (23rd July 2015). *Bloomberg.*
https://www.bloomberg.com/news/articles/2015-07-23/lng-seen-overtaking-iron-ore-as-australia-s-main-export-driver

[17] Commodity Prices, Commodity Currencies, and Global Economic Developments: Working Paper 15743, by Jan J. J. Groen and Paolo A. Pesenti. *National Bureau of Economic Research.* http://www.nber.org/papers/w15743

[18] "The Sugar Casino", by Jonathan Kingsman. (2015). Createspace.

[19] Can Technical Analysis Predict Commodity Price Developments?, by Casper Bek. (August 2013). *Copenhagen Business School.*
http://studenttheses.cbs.dk/bitstream/handle/10417/4222/casper_bek.pdf?sequence=1

[20] What can the oil futures curve tell us about the outlook for oil prices? By Dan Nixon and Tom Smith. *Bank of England Quarterly Bulletin.* (2012 Q1). Bank of England.
http://www.bankofengland.co.uk/publications/Documents/quarterlybulletin/qb120103.pdf

[21] What Do We Learn from the Price of Crude Oil Futures?, by Alquist, Ron and Kilian, Lutz, (November 2007). *CEPR Discussion Paper* No. DP6548.
https://ssrn.com/abstract=1140075

[22] Australia's central bank admits to a big problem, by Greg McKenna. (20th November 2015). *Business Insider.* https://www.businessinsider.com.au/the-rbas-head-of-economic-analysis-just-said-the-rba-is-not-very-good-at-forecasting-commodities-2015-11

[23] "Why Stock Markets Crash: Critical Events in Complex Financial Systems", by Didier Sornette. (2017). Princeton University Press.

[24] Does anyone make accurate geopolitical predictions? By Barbara Mellers and Michael C. Horowitz. (29th January 2015). *Washington Post.*
https://www.washingtonpost.com/news/monkey-cage/wp/2015/01/29/does-anyone-make-accurate-geopolitical-predictions/?utm_term=.94aee28450a6

[25] US election guide to prediction markets and bets, John Authers. (24th October 2016). *Financial Times.* https://www.ft.com/content/dd6a895e-951b-11e6-a1dc-bdf38d484582

[26] Forty Years of Oil Price Fluctuations: Why the Price of Oil May Still Surprise Us, by Christiane Baumeister and Lutz Kilian. *JOURNAL OF ECONOMIC PERSPECTIVES,* VOL. 30, NO. 1, WINTER 2016 (pp. 139-60) https://www.aeaweb.org/articles?id=10.1257/jep.30.1.139

[27] "The Signal and the Noise: The Art and Science of Prediction", by Nate Silver. (2013). Penguin

[28] "Complexity: A Guided Tour", by Melanie Mitchell. (2011). Oxford University Press

[29] "The Alchemy of Finance: Reading the Mind of the Market", George Soros. (1994). John Wiley & Sons

[30] Quantification of the High Level of Endogeneity and of Structural Regime Shifts in Commodity Markets, No. 212, by Vladimir Filimonov, David Bicchetti, Nicolas Maystre and Didier Sornette. (November 2013). *United Nations Conference on Trade and Development (UNCTD)* http://unctad.org/en/PublicationsLibrary/osgdp20132_en.pdf

[31] "Essentials of Petroleum: A Key to Oil Economics", 2nd Revised edition, by Paul Frankel. (2012). Routledge

[32] "Fooled by Randomness: The Hidden Role of Chance in Life and in the Markets", by Nassim Nicolas Taleb. (2007). Penguin

[33] Why Oil Demand May Be Higher Than Expected, by Georgi Kantchev. (17th March 2017). *WSJ* https://www.wsj.com/articles/why-oil-demand-may-be-higher-than-expected-1489730400

[34] Iraq Reveals Oilfields Output to Win Over OPEC Ahead of Meeting, by Sam Wilkin. (30th October 2016). *Bloomberg.* https://www.bloomberg.com/news/articles/2016-10-30/iraq-reveals-oilfields-output-to-win-over-opec-ahead-of-meeting

[35] "Future Babble: Why Expert Predictions Fail - and Why We Believe Them Anyway", Dan Gardner. (2011). Virgin Books

[36] "Why Your World Is About to Get a Whole Lot Smaller: Oil and the End of Globalization", by Jeff Rubin. (2009). Random House

[37] Unskilled and unaware of it: How difficulties in recognising one's own incompetence lead to inflated self-assessments, by Justin Kruger and David Dunning. (1999). *Journal of Personality and Social Psychology,* vol 77, No 6, pp 1121-1134. http://psych.colorado.edu/~vanboven/teaching/p7536_heurbias/p7536_readings/kruger_dunning.pdf

[38] Competing to Be Certain (But Wrong): Market Dynamics and Excessive Confidence in Judgment, by Joseph R. Radzevick and Don A. Moore. *Management Science*, Vol. 57, No. 1 (January 2011), pp. 93-106 http://www.jstor.org/stable/41060703

[39] "The Truth", by Terry Pratchett. (2013). Corgi

[40] "The Black Swan: The Impact of the Highly Improbable", by Nassim Nicholas Taleb. (2008). Penguin

[41] "The Storytelling Animal: How Stories Make Us Human", by Jonathan Gottschall. (2013). Mariner Books

[42] "Narrative Economics", by Robert J. Shiller. (2017). *The National Bureau of Economic Research* http://www.nber.org/papers/w23075

[43] Prior Exposure Increases Perceived Accuracy of Fake News, by Pennycook, Gordon and Cannon, Tyrone D and Rand, David G of Yale University. (July 5, 2017) https://ssrn.com/abstract=2958246

[44] Her real name was Dorothy Martin, but Festinger changed her name in his book to protect her anonymity.

[45] "When Prophecy Fails: A Social and Psychological Study of a Modern Group That Predicted the Destruction of the World", by Leon Festinger, Henry Riecken, Stanley Schachter. (1956). Harper-Torchbooks

[46] "Food Prices", by Max Roser (2016). *OurWorldInData.org*. https://ourworldindata.org/food-prices/

[47] "The Ultimate Resource", by Julian Simon. (1981). Princeton University Press

[48] The next shock? (4th March 2009). *The Economist* http://www.economist.com/node/188181

[49] "The Growth Map: Economic Opportunity in the BRICs and Beyond", by Jim O'Neil. (2011). Portfolio Penguin

[50] Trending Upward: How the intelligence community can better see into the future, by Phillip Tetlock and Michael Horowitz. (7th September 2012). *Foreign Policy*. http://foreignpolicy.com/2012/09/07/trending-upward/

[51] Building Better Global Economic BRICs, by Jim O'Neil. (30th November 2011). *Goldman Sachs* http://www.goldmansachs.com/our-thinking/archive/archive-pdfs/build-better-brics.pdf

[52] The BRICs era is over, even at Goldman Sachs, by Heather Timmons. (9th November 2015). *Quartz* https://qz.com/544410/the-brics-era-is-over-even-at-goldman-sachs/

[53] Why Goldman's Oil Guru Predicts a 'Super Spike', by Louise Story. (21st May 2008). *CNBC* https://www.cnbc.com/id/24750739

[54] New 'super-spike' might mean $200 a barrel oil, by Steve Gelsi. (7th March 2008). *Marketwatch*

[55] After Saying Oil Would "Not Hit $44 During My Lifetime", Gartman Flip-Flops, Turns Bullish, by Tyler Durden. (27th April 2016). *Zero Hedge* http://www.zerohedge.com/news/2016-04-27/after-saying-oil-would-not-hit-44-during-his-lifetime-gartman-flip-flops-turns-bulli

[56] Oil's not going above $55 for years, and here's why: Gartman, by Annie Pei. (7th September 2016). *CNBC*. https://www.cnbc.com/2016/09/07/oils-not-going-above-55-for-years-and-heres-why-gartman.html

[57] James Randi and the Seer-Sucker Illusion. (11th August 2010). *The Psy-Fi Blog*. http://www.psyfitec.com/2010/08/james-randi-and-seer-sucker-illusion.html

[58] Debunking goldbugs, by Izabella Kaminska. (31st May 2012). *FT Alphaville.* https://ftalphaville.ft.com/2012/05/31/1023571/debunking-goldbugs/
[59] "The New Case for Gold", by James Rickards. (2016). Portfolio
[60] "The Big Reset Revised Edition: War on Gold and the Financial Endgame", by Willem Middelkoop. (2015). Amsterdam University Press
[61] LET'S BE HONEST ABOUT GOLD: IT'S A PET ROCK, by Jason Zweig. (17th July 2015). *Jason Zweig* http://jasonzweig.com/lets-be-honest-about-gold-its-a-pet-rock/
[62] The word "whipsaw" comes from the timber industry where a long, thin, two-man wood saw would often get caught in a log, if not properly handled, and whip the sawyers back and forth without cutting the wood and subjecting them to "two damaging and usually opposing forces at the same time".
[63] Beware of Guru Worship – George Soros Edition, by Cullen Roche. (6th September 2016). *Pragmatic Capitalism* http://www.pragcap.com/beware-of-guru-worship/
[64] Priors and Desires: a Model of Optimism,Pessimism, and Cognitive Dissonance, by Guy Mayraz. (2014). *Oxford University Centre for Experimental Social Science* http://www.business.uwa.edu.au/__data/assets/pdf_file/0004/2630335/Guy-Mayraz-Priors-and-Desires-A-Model-of-Optimism-Pessimism-and-Cognitive-Dissonance.pdf
[65] Forecasting metal prices: Do forecasters herd?, by Christian Pierdziocha, Jan-Christoph Rulke and Georg Stadtmann. (September 2012). *European University Viadrina Frankfurt (Oder), Department of Business Administration and Economics.* Discussion Paper No. 325
[66] Security Analyst's Career Concerns and Herding of Investment Forecasts, by Harrison Hong, Jeffrey D. Kubik and Amit Solomon. *RAND Journal of Economics*, Vol. 31, No. 1, Spring 2000, pp. 121–144 http://citeseerx.ist.psu.edu/viewdoc/download?doi=10.1.1.440.7129&rep=rep1&type=pdf
[67] The Market for "Lemons": Quality Uncertainty and the Market Mechanism, by George A. Akerlof. *The Quarterly Journal of Economics*, Vol. 84, No. 3. (Aug., 1970), pp. 488-500. http://www.econ.yale.edu/~dirkb/teach/pdf/akerlof/themarketforlemons.pdf
[68] The Seer-Sucker Theory: The Value of Experts in Forecasting, by Armstrong, J. Scott. (1980). *Technology Review*, pp. 16-24. https://ssrn.com/abstract=648763
[69] "The Signal and the Noise: The Art and Science of Prediction", by Nate Silver. (2013). Penguin
[70] Noise, by Fischer Black. Journal of Finance, Volume 41, Issue 3, Paper and proceeding of the Forty-Fourth Annual Meeting of the Amercia Finance

Association, New York, New York, December 20-30, 1985 (Jul, 1986), 529-543 http://projects.digital-cultures.net/reading-algorithms/files/2016/06/Blac86.pdf

[71] "Future Babble: Why Expert Predictions Fail - and Why We Believe Them Anyway", Dan Gardner. (2011). Virgin Books

[72] "The Little Book of Behavioral Investing: How not to be your own worst enemy", by James Montier. (2010). John Wiley & Sons

[73] Herbert Simon. (20th March 2009). *The Economist* http://www.economist.com/node/13350892

[74] Asiaphoria Meets Regression to the Mean, by Lant Pritchett and Lawrence Summers. (October 2014). *NBER Working Paper* No. 20573 http://www.nber.org/papers/w20573

[75] Playing dice with criminal sentences: the influence of irrelevant anchors on experts' judicial decision making, by Englich B1, Mussweiler T, Strack F. *Personality & Social Psychology Bulletin*. 2006 Feb; 32(2):188-200 https://www.ncbi.nlm.nih.gov/pubmed/16382081

[76] A Mind Is a Terrible Thing to Change: Confirmatory Bias in Financial Markets, by Sebastien Pouget, Julien Sauvagnat and Stephane Villeneuve. *The Review of Financial Studies*, Volume 30, Issue 6, 1 June 2017, Pages 2066–2109, https://doi.org/10.1093/rfs/hhw100

[77] "Black Box Thinking: Marginal Gains and the Secrets of High Performance", by Matthew Syed. (2016). John Murray

[78] An Inconvenient Truth about OPEC, by Anas Alhajji. (15th September 2010). *Project Syndicate* https://www.project-syndicate.org/commentary/an-inconvenient-truth-about-opec?barrier=accessreg

[79] "Irrational Exuberance", by Robert Schiller. (2001). Princeton University Press

[80] The Kinks of Financial Journalism, by Diego Garcia of the *University of Colorado at Boulder*. (2014) http://gsm.ucdavis.edu/sites/main/files/file-attachments/04_the_kinks_of_financial_journalism.pdf

[81] Beyond the Supercycle: How Technology is Reshaping Resources. (February 2017). McKinsey Global Institute. http://www.mckinsey.com/~/media/McKinsey/Business%20Functions/Sustainability%20and%20Resource%20Productivity/Our%20Insights/How%20technology%20is%20reshaping%20supply%20and%20demand%20for%20natural%20resources/MGI-Beyond-the-Supercycle-Full-report.ashx

[82] Morgan Stanley Capital International All Country World Index

[83] "White Elephants" and Other Monetary Ailments, by Marc Faber. (26th June 2003). *Daily Reckoning* https://dailyreckoning.com/white-elephants-and-other-monetary-ailments/

[84] Global Dairy Trade

[85] Chinese demand to drive high dairy prices in 2014. (19th December 2013). *Farming UK* https://www.farminguk.com/News/Chinese-demand-to-drive-

high-dairy-prices-in-2014_27047.html
[86] Dairy Quarterly Q4: dairy pricing set to continue at high levels in 2014 due to Chinese demand. (19th December 2013). *Rabobank* http://rabobank-food-agribusiness-research.pr.co/67118-rabobank-dairy-quarterly-q4-dairy-pricing-set-to-continue-at-high-levels-in-2014-due-to-chinese-demand
[87] Chinese stockpiling curdles New Zealand's milk, by Miles Grafton. (1st April 2016). *Asia and the Pacific Policy Society*. https://www.policyforum.net/chinese-stockpiling-curdles-new-zealands-milk/
[88] Got Milk? Too much of it, say U.S. dairy farmers, Heather Haddon. (21st May 2017). *Market Watch* http://www.marketwatch.com/story/got-milk-too-much-of-it-say-us-dairy-farmers-2017-05-21
[89] Dairy price estimates are consistently wrong, by Keith Woodford (31st May 2016). https://keithwoodford.wordpress.com/2016/05/31/dairy-price-estimates-are-consistently-wrong/
[90] Dairy prices are not predictable, by Keith Woodford. (20th April 2016). https://keithwoodford.wordpress.com/2016/04/20/dairy-prices-are-not-predictable/
[91] Molycorp prospectus. (12th July 2010) p6 https://www.sec.gov/Archives/edgar/data/1489137/000095012310070661/d70469b4e424b4.htm
[92] Oil heads back to $30/bbl and probably lower, by Paul Hodges. (July 2016). The pH Report http://internationalechem.com/wp-content/uploads/2016/08/The-pH-Report-Oil-heads-back-to-30-per-barrel-and-probably-lower-July-2016.pdf
[93] "Commodities: 50 Things You Really Need To Know", by Peter Sainsbury. (2015). Pronoun
[94] The resource curse without natural resources: Expectations of resource booms and their impact, by Jędrzej George Frynas, Geoffrey Wood, Timothy Hinks. Afr Aff (Lond) 2017 1-28. 10.1093/afraf/adx001
[95] Terry-Lynn Karl and Ian Gary, 'The global record', in *Foreign Policy in Focus (Interhemispheric Resource Center/Institute for Policy Studies/SEEN*, Washington, DC and Silver City, NM, 2004), pp. 35–42, p. 36.
[96] Sustaining development in mineral economies: The resource curse thesis, by Richard M. Auty. *Resources Policy*, 1994, vol. 20, issue 1, pp. 77-78 http://econpapers.repec.org/article/eeejrpoli/v_3a20_3ay_3a1994_3ai_3a1_3ap_3a77-78.htm
[97] Anticipating oil: the temporal politics of a disaster yet to come, by Gisa Weszkalnys. (18th March 2014). *The Sociological Review*, Volume 62, pp. 211–235 http://onlinelibrary.wiley.com/doi/10.1111/1467-954X.12130/abstract
[98] How Brazil's China-Driven Commodities Boom Went Bust, by John Lyons and Paul Kierman. (27th August 2015). *WSJ*. https://www.wsj.com/articles/how-brazils-china-driven-commodities-boom-

went-bust-1440728049
[99] "The Growth Map: Economic Opportunity in the BRICs and Beyond", by Jim O'Neil. (2011). Portfolio Penguin
[100] How Brazil's China-Driven Commodities Boom Went Bust, by John Lyons and Paul Kierman. (27th August 2015). *WSJ*.
https://www.wsj.com/articles/how-brazils-china-driven-commodities-boom-went-bust-1440728049
[101] Dreaming with BRICs: The Path to 2050, by Dominic Wilson & Roopa Purushothaman. (1st October 2003). *Goldman Sachs*
http://www.goldmansachs.com/our-thinking/archive/archive-pdfs/brics-dream.pdf
[102] World Bank. 2012. Mongolia - Country partnership strategy for the period FY2013-2017. *World Bank*.
http://documents.worldbank.org/curated/en/512491468286291144/Mongolia-Country-partnership-strategy-for-the-period-FY2013-2017
[103] "Superforecasting: The Art and Science of Prediction", by Philip Tetlock and Dan Gardner. (2016). Random House Books
[104] Sherman Kent and the Profession of Intelligence Analysis. *The Sherman Kent Center for Intelligence Analysis*. Occasional Papers: Volume 1, Number 5, Nov. '02 https://www.cia.gov/library/kent-center-occasional-papers/vol1no5.htm
[105] "Future Babble: Why Expert Predictions Fail - and Why We Believe Them Anyway", by Dan Gardner. (2011). Virgin Books
[106] "Risk, Uncertainty, and Profit", by Frank Knight. (1921). Boston, MA: Hart, Schaffner & Marx; Houghton Mifflin Co.
http://www.econlib.org/library/Knight/knRUP.html
[107] Verification of Forecasts Expressed in Terms of Probability", Glenn W. Brier. (January 1950). *Monthly Weather Review*, Vol 78, Number 1.
https://docs.lib.noaa.gov/rescue/mwr/078/mwr-078-01-0001.pdf
[108] "Black Box Thinking: Marginal Gains and the Secrets of High Performance", by Matthew Syed. (2016). John Murray
[109] Liebreich: A year of hectic change and off-target predictions, Michael Liebreich. (14th December 2016). *Bloomberg New Energy Finance*.
https://about.bnef.com/blog/off-target-renewable-energy-predictions/
[110] Why IEA scenarios should be treated with extreme caution, by Kate Mackenzie. (24th March 2017). *FT Alphaville*.
https://ftalphaville.ft.com/2017/05/24/2189189/guest-post-why-iea-scenarios-should-be-treated-with-extreme-caution/
[111] "Market Wizards: Interviews with Top Traders", by Jack D. Schwager. (2012) Wiley
[112] Stand Firm: Resisting the Self-Improvement Craze, by Svend Brinkmann. (2017). Polity Press
[113] Becoming an Evidence-Based Trader, by Brett Steenbarger. (26th June

2017). *Traderfeed* http://traderfeed.blogspot.co.uk/2017/06/becoming-evidence-based-trader.html

[114] Crude Volatility -- Lessons From History, by Robert McNally. (February 2017). *Energy Intelligence* http://beta.energyintel.com/world-energy-opinion/crude-volatility-lessons-from-history/

[115] Social Media, News Media and the Stock Market, by Peiran Jiao, Andre Veiga and Ansgar Walther. (October 2016). *Oxford University*. https://www.economics.ox.ac.uk/Department-of-Economics-Discussion-Paper-Series/social-media-news-media-and-the-stock-market

[116] Decoding Social Influence and the Wisdom of the Crowd in Financial Trading Network, by Wei Pan, Yaniv Altshuler and Alex (Sandy) Pentland. (2012). *MIT* http://web.media.mit.edu/~yanival/socialcom12.pdf

[117] "The Bed of Procrustes: Philosophical and Practical Aphorisms", by Nassim Nicholas Taleb. (2016). Penguin

[118] "Abnormal Returns: Winning Strategies From the Frontiers of the Investment Blogosphere", by Tadas Viskanta. (2012). McGraw-Hill

[119] "Why Stock Markets Crash: Critical Events in Complex Financial Systems", by Didier Sornette. (2017). Princeton University Press.

[120] "Expert opinion", by Howard Marks. (January 2017). *Oaktree Capital* https://www.oaktreecapital.com/docs/default-source/memos/expert-opinion.pdf?sfvrsn=4

Printed in Poland
by Amazon Fulfillment
Poland Sp. z o.o., Wrocław